Heavenly Citizenship

The Spiritual Alternative to Power Politics

Fred R. Lybrand, Jr.

Take note that the name satan and related names are not capitalized. We choose not to acknowledge him, even to the point of violating grammatical rules.

Treasure House
An Imprint of
Destiny Image
P.O. Box 310
Shippensburg, PA 17257

"For where your treasure is
there will your heart be also." Matthew 6:21

ISBN 1-56043-785-5

For Worldwide Distribution
Printed in the U.S.A.

ii

Contents

"The great aim of ministry is to lead souls to taste of the 'things above,' and then the things below will not only be surpassed, but there will be a sense of dissatisfaction with them. Sometimes one does not know why one is so dissatisfied, but the reason is, one is not in the element that suits one's divine taste."

—J.B. Stoney

iii

Foreword

Some books have something to say that strikes a responsive chord in the heart as well as in the mind of the reader. This is what *Heavenly Citizenship: The Spiritual Alternative to Power Politics* did for me. It expresses a message that has been largely ignored recently. It has a message distinguished by a full appreciation of Christ's present exaltation in Heaven. But in the press among evangelicals for contemporary relevance, we have ignored the reality that the position of our Head is the basis of our contribution on earth. The message is simple: A Christian's Heavenly citizenship provides for his earthly role. Fred Lybrand brings this message to life for our generation with a rich use of illustrations and analogies that speak to today's questions and thoughts. This is a book that ought to be read by Christians who want to live in a distinctive fashion in today's world.

Elliot E. Johnson
Professor of Bible Exposition
Dallas Theological Seminary

Chapter 1

The New Identity

Few of us have had the opportunity to grow up at the feet of a wise man, but many of us have had one sit in our laps. My son Tripp is one of my wise men. As my first born, he is a fresh spring of illustrations, wisdom, and just the right questions to make me stop and think clearly. At four-and-a-half years old he climbed in my lap one day and started talking about the deep things of God.

He looked at me and said, "You know, Dad, I think Jesus can give us more than we can even think." I responded by reading Ephesians 3 where Paul tells us the same thing. I don't know how Tripp notices such things, but he does. He then went on to ask me about the message I was working on.

"Well," I said. "There apparently is new information that suggests that the Dome of the Rock actually is the true Temple spot. Many believe that the Bible teaches that this Temple spot is the future place where Christ will step down upon the earth for the second time to begin the Millennial Kingdom. The Temple will be there." I further explained to Tripp that it is also understood to be the place that Isaac was almost sacrificed by Abraham.

Tripp and I were talking about this when he said, "Isaac didn't die. There was a ram." I said, "That's right." "Why?" he said. And so, I explained to Tripp. "Well, Son, you see, Abraham was the father. He was going to sacrifice his son. That is just like the way God the Father sent His Son to be sacrificed. It also shows that humans need a sacrifice for our sins. God provided a ram instead of Isaac and a lamb instead of us."

"A lamb? I don't see a lamb," Tripp said. I clarified, "Well, the lamb is Christ, the Lamb of God. You see, you should have died, but He died instead, just like Isaac was going to be sacrificed, but the ram was sacrificed instead." Tripp looked at me, and said, "Makes sense." Four-and-a-half years old, and it makes sense.

This story of Tripp illustrates the nature of learning truth. He realized it made sense as far as it could to a four-and-a-half-year-old. The study we're entering into is something that will make sense to your spirit as well.

The New Identity

Consider the example of something we all learned as a child: how to ride a bike. Riding a bike involves several things: balance, speed, pedaling, steering, etc. You can't really create a priority and order to them. They are all necessary. We are looking at a biblical subject that will have dramatic impact on our lives, and possibly our nation...if we believe it, embrace it, and promote it among the saints. Like riding a bike, it needs all of its dimensions to be understood.

There are two basic questions that human beings face without exception. The questions are: "Who am I?" and "What am I good for?" Have you ever asked yourself these questions? Often we excuse a teen or a young adult in order to allow him or her room to find a purpose and meaning for life. We say, "He's traveling Europe, trying to find himself." Sadly, many never find an answer to these questions.

Have you ever asked yourself, "What do I want to be when I grow up?" I often ask when someone comes in for counseling, "What do you want to be when you grow up?" We all wrestle with this question at one time or another. What do you want to be when you grow up? Who are you anyway?

The human search for purpose and meaning is intricately connected to our sense of identity. Identity is crucial to the issue of being a citizen of

Heaven. If I compared it to learning to ride a bike, it would be like saying, "One thing you have to remember about a bike is that you've got to keep it moving, keep it moving." I don't have all the rules of a bike, but I have one: Keep it moving. I remember growing up that, excepting training wheels, you're not riding if you stop...bikes don't stand up very well by themselves.

Identity or identification is similar as it concerns our Heavenly citizenship. If we at least understand the importance of the issue of identity, then we will see how Heaven affects us on a day-to-day basis. This is not to be pie in the sky. This is to be life-changing. Moreover, if you fail to grasp this truth, you will fail to experience Christianity as God intends.

It may be that the impotence of the church in our day stems from an identity crisis. Most of the outspoken leadership in the church today is proclaiming that we've "forgotten what we are supposed to do." Doing will come, but never the right kind before our identity is Heavenly.

There are three important principles regarding identification. First, we must understand the concept. *Identification means that we must find our identity, or a sense of who we are, in some thing, some idea, or some group.* We especially tend to identify with things and people outside of ourselves.

4

The New Identity

The ability and necessity of identification is an undeniable part of being human. That may appear merely theoretical, but it's very practical. I believe it goes back to the Garden of Eden, back to Creation, and back to the image of God and our need for God. It is something so intrinsic to us that it cannot be denied or resisted. We gravitate to it. We are attracted to find identity and to identify with something. The object of identification may vary, but it is unavoidable. It is a part of us. It is part of being human. It's part of being real. Unfortunately, it is also a part of why we're messed up. It is also, surprisingly, how we can get better.

We ask the question, "Who am I?" I've asked that question: Who am I? Well, I'm Fred. That doesn't do much for you, being a Fred. I don't know if you've ever thought of that, but it just doesn't do that much for me, a Fred. I've even had people want to make me a 'Frederick', trying to help me out with my identity. Frederick sounds more noble. Isn't it more victorious, more like a conqueror? But Fred? That doesn't do much for me.

Perhaps I should focus on my last name, Lybrand. Ah, I'm a Lybrand. Well, that's not too helpful either. I can look at the history of the Lybrands. We come from Germany, through England, and who knows where else. We go back to royalty in Germany, but probably a few peasants too. Regardless of our heritage, names are not enough to identify with.

"Who am I?" Perhaps our identity is found in our roles and functions in society. I am a father. I am a graduate of the University of Alabama. What does that do? I graduated from Dallas Theological Seminary. Well, depending on where you are, that does something, or perhaps nothing at all. Our accomplishments cannot provide an adequate sense of identity.

When a young person attends college, there is a tendency, depending on the college, to join a fraternity or a sorority. It identifies the young person with a group of individuals. There is a lengthy and complicated process of becoming identified with one of these organizations on campus. Even being independent of any organization identifies a person. Social organizations we join give us an identity. The schools we attend offer us identity.

The sports teams from these schools often carry with us all of our lives. "I'm a Seminole. I'm an Aggie. I'm a Longhorn." How would you like to be a 'Ramblin Wreck from Georgia Tech'? These are all identity issues, and we say it, depending on how well the sports program's going at the moment, with pride.

It is amazing to me that, regardless of how long one has been away from college, we can be impacted by the score of a football game. Most likely we no longer are acquainted with any of the players. The coaches may have changed. We don't know the trainers. However, we went to school there, and for some reason, whether they win or lose, it will affect us emotionally.

One who attended the competing school would most likely have the exact opposite reaction. It is not logical. Yet, it is a part of us. It is undeniable. We cheer because we have identified ourselves with the team, not because it is morally superior. When we join a club, we get to belong. We get a sense of ownership and identity.

Identity can be determined from thousands of sources. I'm married. I'm single. I'm a parent. I belong to this city. I'm a Texan. I'm an American, proud to be an American. I do this job. Or on the negative side, perhaps I don't have this job. Well, I'm white. I'm black. I'm Hispanic. I'm a Southerner. I'm blue collar. I'm white collar. I'm Christian. I'm Muslim. I'm Mormon. I'm a Baptist. I'm a Methodist. I'm a charismatic. I'm fat. I'm thin. I'm an athlete. I'm an intellectual.

Our lives gravitate toward finding identity. It's part of finding meaning or a sense of belonging. The dynamics are both simple and complex. It's part of the reason why the threat of losing a job hurts so much. It's not just the loss of income or the change in life style, but part of who we perceive ourselves to be is destroyed. It is amazing how intrinsic to our humanness this principle is.

There is something that can happen to us emotionally when our sense of identity is challenged. In many ways, it makes no sense at all. There is a part of every one of us that cannot be denied or restrained, that gravitates to trying to find something to identify with.

There's a second principle surrounding our identity. *There are only two sources for identity: Heaven and earth.* Everything fits under those categories: Heaven and earth. The Gospel of John chapter 3 records John the Baptist speaking of Christ:

> *John answered and said, "A man can receive nothing unless it has been given to him from heaven."* (John 3:27)

John explains that things come from Heaven. He's referring to Christ and where He's from and what He has.

There is a dichotomy in the Word of God. Look at verse 31.

> *He who comes from above is above all; he who is of the earth is earthly and speaks of the earth. He who comes from heaven is above all.* (John 3:31)

John sees a distinction between Heaven and earth. Christ came from Heaven to the earth. Where do you think he got that? Well, I suspect he got it from listening to Christ. Christ said:

If I have told you earthly things and you do not believe, how will you believe if I tell you heavenly things? (John 3:12)

Christ emphasized a dichotomy. All things are either Heavenly or earthly. If you're not going to believe the earthly things, which He alludes are easier to believe, then how are you going to believe Heavenly things when they are communicated to you?

This, by the way, is in the exact context of the most famous of Scriptures:

For God so loved the world that He gave His only begotten Son that whoever believes in Him should not perish but have everlasting life. (John 3:16)

Consider another example:

To them it was revealed that, not to themselves, but to us they [speaking of prophets] *were ministering the things which now have been reported to you through those who have preached the gospel to you by the Holy Spirit sent from heaven—things which angels desire to look into.* (I Peter 1:12)

Observe here that the reference is to the Spirit, but I think it refers to the gospel that was sent from Heaven as well. That knowledge had to come from Heaven. There is Heavenly knowledge. There is a dichotomy here; the message was sent. It was from Heaven, and the Spirit was also. He came and brought a Heavenly message. The message of grace would never be considered from the earth; it had to be sent from Heaven.

First Peter 3:22 says, speaking of Christ in the context, "Who has gone into heaven and is at the right hand of God, angels and authorities and powers having been made subject to Him." Christ is in Heaven and everything is subject to Him from that position. There is a dichotomy in which Heaven is superior. There is a clear distinction between Heavenly things and earthly things.

There is another passage that helps us understand that there are two sources—Heaven and earth—for our identity: James 3:13-18.

Who is wise and understanding among you? Let him show by good conduct that his works are done in the meekness of wisdom. But if you have bitter envy and self-seeking in your hearts, do not boast and lie against the truth. This wisdom does not descend from above, but is earthly, sensual, demonic. For where envy and self-seeking exist, confusion and every evil thing will be there. But the wisdom that is from above is first pure, then peaceable, gentle, willing to yield, full of mercy and good fruits, without partiality and without hypocrisy. Now the fruit of righteousness is sown in peace by those who make peace. (James 3:13-18)

James explained that there is a dividing line for wisdom. There is wisdom from Heaven and there is wisdom from the earth. It is also a dichotomy, a distinction between two never-to-be-blended things.

As we study through this concept of our Heavenly citizenship, we're going to see that our identity is either gained from earth or from Heaven. That's why Heavenly citizenship is so important. There are two sources for identity: Heaven and earth. There's a corollary to this principle. *The quality of the source of our identity is the key.* If your identity is settled on earthly sources, if you derive meaning and identity of who you are from earth, what kind of quality will you have? Earthly? If you derive it from Heaven, what kind of quality will you have there? Heavenly!

Consider an example. Imagine that your identity comes from your stock portfolio. Stock market up. Portfolio up. Identity up. Stock market down. Portfolio down. Identity down. If we find our sense of belonging, purpose, and meaning—our identity—from things that are earthly, temporary, and changing, then our identity is going to ride the waves.

When we identify with Heaven, our sense of belonging, purpose, and meaning is Heavenly. It does not change. It is superior and eternal.

Have you ever heard this phrase, "Well, you're so Heavenly minded that you're no earthly good"? Where would you find that in the Bible? Let's invert it. "You're so earthly minded that you're no Heavenly good." That's biblical and good theology. Someone turned it around to make the doctrine of Heaven hidden to us because someone knew that it would change us.

There is a third and final principle surrounding our identity. *The essence of authentic Christianity is the change of identity from earth to Heaven.* Authentic Christianity involves us changing from having an earthly identity to a Heavenly one. The principle of identification cannot be denied or resisted, but for the Christian it can be properly directed. A wonderful illustration in the Word of God is childhood to adulthood.

Remember when you finally realized, gentlemen, that you were a man? I don't know if women do this about womanhood, but guys do this. Perhaps it was the first time you broke some barrier. Maybe it was the amount you paid the government or when you disciplined your child for the first time. Often we see ourselves as men when we get married...it could be anything. There is a point that we come to and finally say, "I'm a man!" That is what growth is. It is childhood as it is meant to be, not wanting to stay a child, but wanting to grow to an adult. It is letting go of the identity of being a child to embrace the identity of being an adult. First Corinthians 13 reads, "When I was a child, I spoke as a child, I understood as a child, I thought as a child; but when I became a man, I put away childish things" (I Cor. 13:11).

12

The New Identity

Doesn't this parallel spiritual growth? When I was an unbeliever, when I was of the earth, when I had the earth in me, I spoke and acted as the earth. But as I grew toward Heaven, in my identity in Christ, I put away earthly things.

The essence of authentic Christianity is the change of identity from earth to Heaven, called growth. However, spiritual growth is limited to the identity we embrace. For example, is it more important to you to be an American or a Christian? I hate to be the one to point out that they are not equal. They never were. Is it more important to be a 'Ramblin Wreck' or a Christian? Is it more important to be wealthy or a believer? Is it more important to be a 'good old boy' and to be liked, or to be a Christian? Is it more important to be a mother or a Christian, a father or a Christian? How about a sports fan or a believer?

Is it more important to be accepted by other people or to be accepted by God as His child?

As long as we embrace an earthly identity, we are limited in our spiritual growth. We are headed to Heaven. Our identity is there. We are citizens of Heaven. We are to grow in finding our identity completely in being Christians.

How do we apply our Heavenly identity? Applying this truth follows a simple formula: understanding plus embracing equals application.

Heavenly identity is not asking you to "do" anything. Instead, the principle of identity is so powerful that if you understand your identity and embrace it, you will change. You'll change like you did when you started school, or joined a club, or heard, "Lybrands don't do that."

This principle of identity is so essential to what you are as a human being that, if you understand and embrace your identity in Heaven, your life must change. Indeed, if it is true on the human level, how much more on the Heavenly one? What we illustrate with human examples hardly compares with the Heavenly reality. Embracing the truth of your Heavenly identity is simply exercising faith. It is faith in what God tells us about our identity through His Word. It is believing what God says is true over all other thoughts, feelings, or opinions.

Second Corinthians 5:17 is one of the first two verses I ever memorized as a believer. "Therefore, if anyone is in Christ, he is a new creation; old things have passed away; behold, all things have become new." Those of us who have come out of backgrounds that have been difficult and devastating, or who have fallen into such insanity and sin that we want a new start, are tremendously touched by this verse. It proves that there is a new start, a new creation. This verse is addressing our position and our identity, though many have confused it with our whole being.

The New Identity

We are new creations in Christ. Ultimately, when we get to Heaven, with a new body and all the rest, we'll be fully new creations. This passage is not speaking of our final state, but our positional one. In fact, I can show this verse is not saying that we are completely new beings once we know Christ. "Old things have passed away; behold, all things have become new." Look at your hand. Is that new? No, that's old. Old creation. Wasting away. Fallible. Flawed. It will die; it will go to dust. The passage means that we're completely new creations, and everything's new, but it is referring to our identity in Christ. No doubt there are spiritual changes within, but that is not the real focus here.

We are new creations and we'll grow up into that. All those things will be put off and all things will become new, but our identity as beings is different. If you know Christ, you are a new creation in the eyes of God. And He, according to Romans 8:28 and 29, is in the process of working out and growing you up in that newness. There's a new start, a new destiny, a new future, and even, in a way, a new past. Your past effectively does not exist; it's forgotten. If you grow up in that differentness, it will prove to be all the more true. You have a new identity.

When you trusted Christ, you became something different than what you were, and what you would have continued to become. Reflect on the fact that we're new creations for a moment. If you reflect and believe this truth just a little, doesn't something feel good about it? Hopeful? Encouraging? It's because the power of truth in combination with this need for identity touches the spiritual center of humanity. It isn't that it "feels good"; it is good. It is a taste of your real identity as a citizen of Heaven and a child of God. Embracing your identity in Him by faith is a Spirit-led look at the real you.

> *For this you know, that no fornicator, unclean person, nor covetous man, who is an idolater, has any inheritance in the kingdom of Christ and God. Let no one deceive you with empty words, for because of these things the wrath of God comes upon the sons of disobedience. Therefore do not be partakers with them. For you were once darkness, but now you are light in the Lord. Walk as children of light.* (Ephesians 5:5-8)

Paul is addressing Christians and warning them not to partake with those of the world in earthly things. You have a new identity. You were once in darkness like them, and partaking with them and their horrendous sin made sense, but now you are light in the Lord. It makes no sense. Walk as children of the light.

If I lived around dogs from an early age and thought I was a dog, I could go out and get on Main

Street on my knees, froth at the mouth, bark, yelp, and chase cars. I'm not a dog, but I'm living up to a false identity.

The Word of God says that, whether or not you feel it or realize it, if you know Christ, you are light in the Lord. You are no longer in darkness. You have a different identity. It's not that God's going to be wonderfully pleased by your righteous walk. It's that a righteous walk only makes sense because you really are light, not darkness. You are a new creation.

Imagine that you have just opened your eyes in a hospital. They tell you that you are recovering from a coma. You have amnesia. Nothing looks familiar. Nothing makes sense. They begin a process with you of showing you pictures of your family, pictures of relatives, pictures of friends, letters you've written, and pictures of where you live. You're hoping, and they're hoping, that maybe something, somehow, will give you that sense of recognition. You have a spouse that you're supposed to love and be married to, but there's no feeling there.

I personally believe that the world has done that to us. We don't know who we are. We are confused. We take up this photo album of the Bible and it shows us these wonderful things about ourselves, yet it does not seem to fit. It looks unfamiliar. It's unclear. It is just like amnesia. If you will hang in there, and study who you are in Christ, something in your heart will rise up and say, "Yes, I belong to Heaven!" There is an unimaginable freedom that will appear in your life as God enables you to shift your identity from this wasting-away world to Heaven, where you belong.

Chapter 2

The New Citizenship

In order to understand our Heavenly citizenship, we can take a look at what citizenship means on a national level. What does it mean to be an American? This question has two answers. The first focuses on our point in time relative to all nations. The second answer focuses on our own history as a nation.

What does it mean to be an American in this present day? It means to be held in contempt by a great portion of the world. We're not always sure why. It is curious that we would still be seen as prosperous in the midst of a recession. However, most of the countries of the world would love to have recessions like ours, compared to what they experience daily.

Many Americans at this moment in time suffer a certain amount of embarrassment with issues like abortion, racial unrest, and the massive and confusing rhetoric of the multi-varied political action groups. If you just consider the current sliver of time, most of us would admit that America has problems. To be an American means to be a part of a great country with great problems.

Our national heritage stirs deeper feelings than the contemporary issues. To be an American is to look back over history and see independent colonies established to allow freedom of religion. There were other issues of noble character that led to the revolutionary war against Great Britain. Early Americans sacrificed a great deal. They survived and began a new republic.

The Constitution is a unique document. We are a unique nation. We have weathered a civil war, World War I, and World War II. America has played an important part in the recent history of peace.

The history of America includes the important role of taking her wealth, converting it, and spreading the message of the gospel to all the world through missionary enterprises. When we think of what it means to be an American, we realize that it means everything in her history. It doesn't stop there; being American includes the future. The more hopeful the future, the better.

Our identity, our source of worth and object of focus, be it a school, state, nation, or family, intimately affects us. The history of our circumstances relates to our identity. Some can research their history to find that they are related to royalty. For some reason, this information affects us in a positive way. You may feel better and stand taller because you are of royal heritage.

The future is also central to the identity issue. If you identify with something outside yourself that has no future, then your identity is diminished. For example, a few years ago, to be a communist in the Soviet Union meant something more positive in that land than it does today. But there's no future in it right now. It might return, but presently it is no longer acceptable to be identified as a communist. Also, if we see a gloomy future for America, it is hard to appreciate identifying ourselves as Americans.

In understanding the issue of Heavenly citizenship it is vital to understand the history of what it means to be a citizen of Heaven. It is important to understand where we have come from and where we are going, just as it is important to understand our history and future as Americans. The context of our history and future allows us to unlock and understand a great portion of the Word of God.

Ephesians 2 gives us much of our history. If you don't understand your history as a citizen of Heaven, it is difficult to appreciate and embrace the life-changing identity that God offers.

Therefore remember that you, once Gentiles in the flesh—who are called Uncircumcision by what is called the Circumcision made in the flesh by hands—that at that time you were without Christ, being aliens from the commonwealth of Israel and strangers from the covenants of promise, having no hope and without God in the world. But now in Christ Jesus you who once were far off have been made near by the blood of Christ. For He Himself is our peace, who has made both one, and has broken down the middle wall of division between us, having abolished in His flesh the enmity, that is, the law of commandments contained in ordinances, so as to create in Himself one new man from the two, thus making peace, and that He might reconcile them both to God in one body through the cross, thereby putting to death the enmity. And He came and preached peace to you who were afar off and those who were near. For through Him we both have access by one Spirit to the Father. Now, therefore, you are no longer strangers and foreigners, but fellow citizens with the saints and members of the household of God. (Ephesians 2:11-19)

This passage embodies some very important truths and considerations in understanding both our Heavenly citizenship and how it changes us. There are three things to consider in this passage. First of all, we were foreigners. The emphasis is on the past.

> *That at that time you were without Christ, being aliens from the commonwealth of Israel and strangers from the covenants of promise, having no hope and without God in the world.* (Ephesians 2:12)

The concept here is that there are two countries, the country of the world and the country of Heaven. Israel, initially, was established on earth as God's representative of this Heavenly country. It was God's representative to offer not only the Seed, the Messiah, but God Himself. The nations would hear of the God of Israel, this Jehovah God, and they would come. The Queen of Sheba came to hear from Solomon about this God. This is the context for Israel. Unfortunately, it was a situation with Israel at the center, while all those outside of Israel were excluded.

There were Gentiles, or in some cases, mixed races, that were not within Israel. They were without God and without hope. The proper way they could come to God would be to convert to Judaism. Paul says of the Gentiles, of which most of us were, that we were aliens from this commonwealth. We were strangers to the covenants of promise—the covenants and the promise to Abraham and David. These things were foreign to us.

These promises, when we were outside of the context of Israel, had nothing to offer us. They were not made to us. We were estranged. We were foreigners. We lived in a different country. It would be just like living in China today. A Chinese citizen gets no benefit from the American Constitution. It doesn't apply.

That was our context. Let me ask you this question. What was this country, our former country, like before we came to Christ? Our former country was the world.

And you He made alive, who were dead in trespasses and sins, in which you once walked according to the course of this world, according to the prince of the power of the air, the spirit who now works in the sons of disobedience, among whom also we all once conducted ourselves in the lust of our flesh, fulfilling the desires of the flesh and of the mind, and were by nature children of wrath, just as the others. (Ephesians 2:1-3)

What was this former country like? It was made up of citizens who were enslaved to their own desires. Paul develops this a little more.

This I say, therefore, and testify in the Lord, that you should no longer walk as the rest of the Gentiles walk, in the futility of their mind, having their understanding darkened, being

24

alienated from the life of God, because of the ignorance that is in them, because of the hardening of their heart; who, being past feeling, have given themselves over to licentiousness, to work all uncleanness with greediness. But you have not so learned Christ. (Ephesians 4:17-20)

What was this foreign country like? It was made up of citizens who were futile in their thinking. They had no understanding. They had a certain arrogance and ignorance in them. They had a hardened heart, a sense of rightness. Yet, they were slaves. The dynamics of the Gentile world of that time weren't much different from our own...we just keep it a little more secret than they did. It was a country of evil. It was a country without love. It was a country with selfishness and self-indulgence. What was our former country like?

Where do wars and fights come from among you? Do they not come from your desires for pleasure that war in your members? You lust and do not have. You murder and covet and cannot obtain. You fight and war. Yet you do not have because you do not ask. You ask and do not receive, because you ask amiss, that you may spend it on your pleasures. Adulterers and adulteresses! Do you not know that

friendship with the world is enmity with God?
Whoever therefore wants to be a friend of the
world makes himself an enemy of God. (James
4:1-4)

What was our former country like? Made up of
citizens who lust, who ask amiss, who war and fight
from selfishness, who because of their friendship
with the world, make themselves enemies of God.
Though this passage in James is addressed to Christians, its rebuke comes from the fact that they were
carrying on as the world.

Do not love the world or the things in the
world. If anyone loves the world, the love of
the Father is not in him. For all that is in the
world—the lust of the flesh, the lust of the
eyes, and the pride of life—is not of the Father
but is of the world. And the world is passing
away, and the lust of it; but he who does the
will of God abides forever. (I John 2:15-17)

What was this former country like? Lust of the
flesh, lust of the eye, pride, arrogance—things not of
God. Boasting, doing what's right in our own eyes. We
had our rights. We knew what was best. We did it
our way. We did not seek advice or counsel. Human
beings were the measure of everything. These are
the rights of a citizen of the world, of a world that,
the apostle John says, is passing away.

The New Citizenship

Let's return to Ephesians, and consider this question: How did we become foreigners? How did we belong to that other country? How did we become foreigners to God and His Heaven? It was very simple. We were born into it. We were born into this sinful state. We are born into this world system, this cosmos. Being born in the world is very much like being born into Nazi Germany. If that was all you knew, if that was all you were taught, if that was all you had, it would stand to reason you would grow up to identify with and be a part of Nazi Germany. What basis would you have to say, "I think there's something wrong with this?"

It is even worse because in this former country of ours, the world, we were born with a tendency to love it. We call it sin. There has been much debate through the years as to whether people are basically good or basically bad. It doesn't really matter because some bad corrupts the whole. For example, the drinking water in my town of Midland, Texas, is basically good, but I don't drink it. It tastes bad and is mineral-ladened. I drink purified water.

We can say people are basically good. That's fine. Yet they still have bad and it corrupts the whole. We are sinners. You are a sinner. It's part of the birthright of the former country. We became foreigners by being born into the world apart from the family

27

of God. Worse than that, we have something inside us that influences us to be like the world. We grew up and said to hatred, anger, and self, "Yes, that feels right, because I'm a citizen of this world." However, something changed according to Ephesians 2:13.

We changed countries. When we, through the work of God, came to a point of ceasing to love ourselves and trust ourselves and realized that there was something wrong, that our destiny was something less than what we had hoped, we came to a point of need and changed countries. We became citizens of a new country called Heaven. Notice verse 13, "But now [contrasted to before] in Christ Jesus you who once were far off have been made near by the blood of Christ." We are near by the blood of Christ. It goes on that He is our peace (v. 14). He has made both one, the Jew and the Gentile. He has done away with those distinctions.

He broke down the middle wall of division. I understand this to be (from verse 13) the wall of commandments, the Mosaic system. He created one new man from the two. This is the Church. He made peace. Christ reconciled everyone who would trust Him to God, making a whole new citizenship. A new country called Heaven. God, in creating the Church, did not thrust us into the old system for Israel, even with its privileges. Nor did He end the future for Israel, since He will fulfill His promises someday. He created a new "country" in the Church, and has given to her a glorious set of privileges and responsibilities of her own.

What is this new country like? Ephesians 2:4-7 reads:

> *But God, who is rich in mercy, because of His great love with which He loved us, even when we were dead in trespasses* [even, you might say, when we were citizens of that other country], *made us alive with Christ (by grace you have been saved), and raised us up together, and made us sit together in the heavenly places in Christ Jesus, that in the ages to come He might show the exceeding riches of His grace in His kindness toward us in Christ Jesus.* (Ephesians 2:4-7)

We find that this new country is Heaven. It is centered on a future. It will involve God's display of His kindness to us who are citizens of this new and glorious country. What is this new country like? This new country, without developing it in the passages, is marked with people who love one another, who belong to this Heavenly country, who are like Christ, who manifest His character, and who let go of being right all the time and embrace being righteous, humble, and authentic before God.

> *But the day of the Lord will come as a thief in the night, in which the heavens will pass away with a great noise, and the elements will*

melt with fervent heat; both the earth and the works that are in it will be burned up. (II Peter 3:10)

This world will not last forever. It will end in destruction. *Since the world is only temporary, we must begin to see ourselves as citizens of that which is eternal. Our lives and our conduct must reflect our new citizenship rather than the old worldly identity.*

Therefore, since all these things will be dissolved, what manner of persons ought you to be in holy conduct and godliness, looking for and hastening the coming of the day of God, because of which the heavens will be dissolved being on fire, and the elements will melt with fervent heat? Nevertheless, we [citizens], *according to His promise, look for new heavens and a new earth in which righteousness dwells. Therefore, beloved, looking forward to these things, be diligent to be found by Him in peace, without spot and blameless.* (II Peter 3:11-14)

What will our new country be like? It will be a place without sin. It will be a place where all the wrongs will be righted.

Some may say, "If this world is the best God can do, He must be flawed too. Therefore, I don't believe in God because of the evil in the world." They misunderstand one point. This is not the best of all possible worlds, but it's the best way to the best of all possible worlds.

God knew all the options. And He decided that, through making man, providing choice, the fall, redemption in Christ, and the pain and suffering in the world, the creation thus (Rom. 8:22) groans, longs to be clothed, changed. This way is the way to the best of all possible worlds. I'm not sure why, but it may have something to do with the contrast of how all the wrongs were righted, and the contrast of seeing what evil was like. We can see at what price and through what means righteousness came, when we will at last arrive in this new country, this new Heaven, to which we are called.

The world focuses on the past and the present and has no future. Yet, our Heavenly country has both a present and a future. The world tends to be natural. Our country is supernatural. The world is evil. Our country is righteous. The world is temporary. Ours is lasting. It is a different country. It is a new country in which righteousness dwells.

Christ Himself came and died an unjust death for us. He offered Himself freely; stripped, beaten, and nailed to a cross. He gave His own life by His own choice, so that God could pour His wrath out upon Christ...never having to pour it out on us. Christ was eternal. He could pay the debt once for all. Otherwise, we would pay for our sins with our suffering existence forever. An eternal God is not satisfied by a temporary sacrifice; therefore, He demanded Christ, the eternal sacrifice, to die for us.

We must not trust in anything except that Christ's death is enough. His death took your sin off you and placed it on Christ. How does this relate to our Heavenly citizenship? We become citizens through the new birth. You have to be born into this new country. It's fallen on hard times, the phrase itself, but the truth has always been there. John 3:7 reads, "You must be born again."

In America, foreigners come to our country, live here for a set time, receive training, learn the language, pass a test, and make a pledge, in order to be naturalized citizens. We, as citizens of Heaven, are super-naturalized, not by our efforts, but by simple faith. What a difficult thing for sinful and prideful people to do! It is hard to let go of any contribution and just embrace a gift. Many think it humiliating to say, "There's nothing I can do to earn God's favor except believe that Christ died, was buried, and was raised for me." Yet, that is exactly how it happens. That's how we become citizens of Heaven.

When we were born again as citizens of Heaven, we became foreigners to our former country. We were foreigners to God, citizens of the world. We became citizens of God's country, and, as a result, we have become foreigners to our former country.

The New Citizenship

The Bible, in many places, calls us to live as strangers, aliens, and pilgrims in this world. It makes sense that there is a perfect dichotomy, a perfect either/or, in this concept. If I'm a citizen of one country and give up, defect from that country, and embrace another one, then I am a foreigner to the first one. It must be that way. Christ was the one who said, "If you're not with Me, you're against Me" (see Lk. 11:23).

There is no place for anyone to be neutral. We must be either a citizen of Heaven or a citizen of the world. The two are diametrically opposed to one another, and there is no place in between where a person can sit. There is no neutral state between the Kingdom of the Son of His love and the world. There is no third option.

Some argue that we are dual citizens, belonging to both Heaven and our earthly country. Another volume is needed to exhaustively examine this issue. For our purposes, however, I believe the Bible teaches that there is no real duality. The Bible teaches a sole citizenship in Heaven and a pilgrimage for us as strangers on earth. We are to submit to governments, but only because it shows forth the character of the God we serve and our trust in Him.

If it somehow could be shown that Christians belong to these two nations, then another principle from our Lord prevails: "No one can serve two masters" (Mt. 6:24). Which country will be superior? If your earthly country is elevated to an equal or superior status to Heaven, then it effectively becomes your only country. Once your earthly nation becomes your master, then the battles you fight and the concerns you embrace will shift. Worse yet, the way in which you read your Bible and serve the Lord will be shaped toward earth and away from Heaven.

John chapter 17, you may remember, records Christ's high priestly prayer. He prayed for Himself and His disciples. Notice the contrast between belonging to the world and belonging to God.

Jesus spoke these words, lifted up His eyes to heaven, and said: "Father, the hour has come. Glorify Your Son, that Your Son also may glorify You, as You have given Him authority over all flesh, that He should give eternal life to as many as You have given Him. And this is eternal life, that they may know You, the only true God, and Jesus Christ whom You have sent. I have glorified You on the earth. I have finished the work which You have given Me to do. And now, O Father, glorify Me together with Yourself, with the glory which I had with You before the world was. I have manifested Your name to the men whom You have given Me out of the world. They were Yours, You gave them to Me, and they have kept Your word. Now they have known that all things which You have given Me are from You. For I have given to them the words which You have given Me; and they have received them, and have known surely that I came forth from You;

and they have believed that You sent Me. I pray for them. I do not pray for the world but for those whom You have given Me, for they are Yours. And all Mine are Yours, and Yours are Mine, and I am glorified in them. Now I am no longer in the world, but these are in the world, and I come to You. Holy Father, keep through Your name those whom You have given Me, that they may be one as We are. While I was with them in the world, I kept them in Your name. Those whom You gave Me I have kept; and none of them is lost except the son of perdition [Judas], that the Scripture might be fulfilled. But now I come to You, and these things I speak in the world, that they may have My joy fulfilled in themselves. I have given them Your word; and the world has hated them because they are not of the world, just as I am not of the world. I do not pray that You should take them out of the world, but that You should keep them from the evil one. They are not of the world, just as I am not of the world. Sanctify them by Your truth. Your word is truth. As You sent Me into the world, I also have sent them into the world. And for their sakes I sanctify Myself, that they also may be sanctified by the truth." (John 17:1-19)

Again, there's a tremendous dichotomy here that once we belong to Him, just as He is not of the world, neither are we. The world will hate us. That's okay. We've been prayed for to be kept. Do you think God will honor Christ's prayer? If He's going to listen to

35

any prayer, surely He'll listen to His own Son's. He prayed to keep us.

We became foreigners the day we became citizens of Heaven. *We became foreigners to the world and its corrupt system. When we live under its rules and indulge in its practices, belong to it and embrace it, not simply appropriately adapting to a situation; when it takes root in our souls, we are living a betrayal of our Heavenly citizenship.*

Each of us must choose our nation. You will live a life consistent with the country that is your identity. If you choose worldly citizenship, the world has to be anesthesia, a pain killer, to you, because you have nothing else. You will also be burdened to protect it and fight for it, just as the alcoholic guards and serves his next drink.

Instead, I'd rather call to you, "Come home." You may have yielded to the allure of the world. You may be waking up and finding that you have been living as a citizen of a country to which you do not belong. You may have forgotten that you're a citizen of Heaven. Come back home.

Finally, some of you are foreigners to Heaven. Some of you are still struggling with belonging to the world. Some of you still have not decided to defect and become a traitor to the world. The Lord wants you to belong to His Heaven. The Lord wants you to give up on your old citizenship, on your old country. He's calling out to offer you a new start and a new identity. What are you waiting for? It's a great country, but He won't wait forever. Trust in Christ rather than yourself and receive the Heavenly citizenship God has destined for you, if you believe.

Chapter 3

The New Life

When I was in the eleventh grade I broke a bone in my hand called the metacarpal. I'm not proud of this, particularly because it is rather stupid to hit people on the side of the head. Our assistant principal at school had fallen through the ceiling. I told others that I saw him fall. One individual called me a liar. I ran that through my personality and didn't respond well, and, as he began to turn, I swung and caught him on the side of the head, snapping the bone in my hand. They call it a boxer's break, but I'm no boxer.

This fellow was so disliked that the doctor didn't charge me. He was happy that someone had hit this kid. This young man was always in trouble and often in the way. Six weeks later, my broken bone was healed. This event typifies how one can have the right enemy but the wrong solution. Ideally, I should have walked away, turned the other cheek, or corrected him. Any of those options would have been fine. My response was to hit him.

Do you know what your biggest enemy is? If you do know what your biggest enemy is, do you know the right way to deal with that enemy? If you are whaling away at the side of the head of your enemy with your fist, you're just going to get hurt and get very little accomplished. We need to recognize our biggest enemy, and know the proper solution to dealing with that enemy.

I'm afraid many of us treat our biggest enemy very much like we treat cancer. Cancer is a very serious disease. Many of us will have members of our family who will face cancer. Almost no one is exempted. The curious thing about cancer is that it is a common phenomenon for people to be concerned that they may have cancer, yet not be examined by a doctor. In fact, they just keep refusing to go to the doctor until they are finally forced to go. Often this is too late. It can't be treated because it wasn't caught at an early stage.

Some people simply do not want to know. I suppose the idea is, "If I pretend I don't have it, or if I don't look at it, then maybe I don't." Common sense tells us that it is much better to deal with the disease than to deny the possibility.

The same concept applies regarding our common enemy. It is better to face it and deal with it rather than pretend the problem isn't there. I fear greatly that most of us just pretend.

What is our biggest enemy? Romans 3:10 and 11 explains, "As it is written: 'There is none righteous, no, not one; there is none who understands; there is none who seeks after God.'" The greatest enemy of mankind is sin. Sometimes people ignore and deny sin.

> *"They have all gone out of the way; they have together become unprofitable; there is none who does good, no, not one. Their throat is an open tomb; with their tongues they have practiced deceit; The poison of asps is under their lips; Whose mouth is full of cursing and bitterness. Their feet are swift to shed blood; destruction and misery are in their ways; and the way of peace they have not known. There is no fear of God before their eyes."* (Romans 3:12-18)

Our biggest enemy is sin. Satan is certainly an enemy. However, if he doesn't have sin to work with, he can't do much to us. Take care of the sin issue, and he will be in desperate trouble. What if I advertised a sermon as follows: "Everybody come to church. Fred's speaking on sin today." Even my fellow elders might say, "I think I'll scalp my yard today." We don't like to hear about sin. There is something in us that hates to face and discuss the sin issue.

What struggles do you personally face right now? I'm not referring to sin necessarily, just struggles in life. Some may be facing health concerns. Some are facing things that have happened at work. Others are affected by relationship struggles, or an absence of relationship struggles. What kind of struggles are you facing internally? Are there things that no one knows about? Everyone struggles.

When we come to church, we dress up and make ourselves presentable. We look nice. We comb our hair. We try to make ourselves look great. We sit in our pews. Sometimes we take notes. It looks good, but we are still in pain. It may be hard to recognize in this setting, but everyone has scars and all of us are struggling. How much of our struggles are made worse because of sin?

My experience has been that troubles are always worsened by how we react, and we usually react with a shade of sin. John 8 is a wonderful illustration of how blinding sin is, and how important it is to be set free. John 8:21 reads, "Then Jesus said to them again, 'I am going away, and you will seek Me, and will die in your sin. Where I go you cannot come.'"

So the Jews said, "Will He kill Himself, because He says, 'Where I go you cannot come'?" And He said to them, "You are from beneath; I am from above. You are of this world; I am not of this world. Therefore I said to you that you will die in your sins; for if you do not believe that I am He, you will die in your sins." Then [sidestepping the issue] *they said to Him, "Who are You?" And Jesus said to them, "Just what I have been saying to you from the beginning. I have many things to say and to judge concerning you, but He who sent Me is true; and I speak to the world those things which I heard from Him." They did not understand that He spoke to them of the Father. Then Jesus said to them, "When you lift up the Son of Man, then you will know that I am He, and that I do nothing of Myself; but as My Father taught Me, I speak these things. And He who sent Me is with Me. The Father has not left Me alone for I always do those things that please Him." As He spoke these words, many believed in Him.* (John 8:22-30)

This sets the context for something very amazing. "Then Jesus said to those Jews who believed Him, 'If you abide in My word, you are My disciples indeed. And you shall know the truth, and the truth shall make you free'" (Jn. 8:31-32).

Notice verse 33: "They answered Him." "They" refers back to the Jews He's having this dialogue with, the Pharisees. "They answered Him, 'We are Abraham's descendants, and have never been in bondage to anyone. How can You say, "You will be made free"?' "

Here is a group of men whose focus is on the fact that though they are blind they believe they are free. Think about it. They were under Roman domination. They had a whole history of captivities. They had been slaves scattered throughout the world. When they addressed Jesus, they were not politically free. Yet they claimed, "We've never been in bondage to anyone." This is an example of blind denial. They did not face the facts. How much of the Pharisees' problem stemmed from the sin of self-righteousness? A great portion.

That kind of blindness is of the sort that could make me break my hand on the side of someone's head and be angry at the person for it happening. This is the kind of blindness that allows us to not go and get checked for cancer when we suspect that we could have the disease.

This chapter deals with how to be free. We all struggle and need to find freedom in Christ.

There is an incorrect way to try to free ourselves from sin. Oftentimes, we try to set personal goals not to sin. Trying not to sin is the wrong answer. *If your goal regarding sin is to not sin, then you have missed the solution.* Dead people in cemeteries do not sin. They are not sinning because they are not living.

The New Life

There was a poster at my college with a logical argument on it. It was a picture of a gorilla with a beer in his hand. The inscription read, "When I drink, I get drunk. When I get drunk, I sleep. When I sleep, I don't sin. If I don't sin, I go to Heaven. So let's all drink and go to Heaven."

It is amazing to me how confused we get. The issue is not to not sin. Dead people don't sin. That is not the goal. If we get caught up in trying not to sin we will most certainly sin. When we try not to focus on something, we focus on it. When we try to focus on not sinning, it has the same effect. If you have a problem with anger, have you ever tried this: "I'm not going to get mad. I'm not going to get mad. I'm not going to GET MAD!!!" What happens? You explode. We are trapped by sin when we think the goal is to not sin. Pledging to not sin is simply the creation of a law from yourself. Law will no more stop sin for you than it did for the Pharisees (Gal. 2:21).

Our true goal is to become righteous, to become Christlike. When we are living godly lives, we are not sinning as a result. Consider the relationship between drowning and swimming. If you want to drown-proof your child, teach the child to swim. There is no such thing as anti-sinking lessons. If you focus on not sinking, you're not focusing on the right thing. Teach the child to swim. When you are swimming, you are not sinking.

The way to walk on a balance beam is to look at the end of it. That focus allows you to traverse the space and walk the distance. The right solution to the sin problem is to become righteous.

There are two kinds of righteousness that must concern us. The first is what we call a declared righteousness. It is similar to or seen in Romans 5:1. It says, "Therefore, having been justified by faith, we have peace with God through our Lord Jesus Christ." The word "justified" there has traditionally and correctly carried the meaning associated with our standing. When we justify the columns on a typewriter or a computer, they all go to one side and they all line up perfectly. This declared righteousness is when we are brought under and line up under God and His will through Christ. It means that God has declared us legally, positionally, and judicially to be righteous in His eyes.

When Christ died on the cross, He took our unrighteousness off of us and put it on Himself. His sacrifice gives us right standing before God, so that when He sees those who know Christ, He sees righteousness. He declared it so. It's very similar to playing tag or hide-and-go-seek, or any of these childhood games. Something is declared "base." It is a place of safety. In and of itself it does not deserve to be base; it has no magic. But once you declare it and touch it, you are safe. The Lord Jesus, when we trust Him, because God has said so, declares us righteous and safe. It doesn't matter if you feel it or not. If you trust in Christ alone, it is true, you are righteous in His eyes.

However, there is a second kind of righteousness. It is the righteousness that is experienced. The kind we grow in. The kind that is worked out through us, such that we live out godliness and righteousness. It is not a self-righteous performance, but a God-righteous change from the inside out.

Often, the missing key is Heavenly citizenship, the fact that we belong to Heaven. We are aliens here. We belong to another country that we are destined for someday. We are ambassadors for and citizens of our Heavenly home. That fact is foundational to our walk in righteousness. The degree to which you do not understand your citizenship will in large measure affect how well you're going to be able to walk in righteousness.

The Bible intimately links our righteousness and our Heavenly citizenship. Second Corinthians 5:17-21 reads:

> *Therefore, if anyone is in Christ, he is a new creation; old things have passed away; behold, all things have become new. Now all things are of God, who has reconciled us to Himself through Jesus Christ, and has given us the*

ministry of reconciliation, that is, that God was in Christ reconciling the world to Himself, not imputing their trespasses to them, and has committed to us the word of reconciliation. Therefore we are ambassadors for Christ, as though God were pleading through us: we implore you on Christ's behalf, be reconciled to God. For He made Him who knew no sin to be sin for us, that we might become the righteousness of God in Him. (II Corinthians 5:17-21)

The Word of God refers to our Heavenly citizenship, or the concept of our identity in Him, and then immediately addresses living righteous lives again and again. The whole context of this new creation has to do with our becoming the righteousness of God in Christ.

But God, who is rich in mercy, because of His great love with which He loved us, even when we were dead in trespasses, made us alive together with Christ (by grace you have been saved), and raised us up together, and made us sit together in the heavenly places in Christ Jesus, that in the ages to come He might show the exceeding riches of His grace in His kindness toward us in Christ Jesus. For by grace you have been saved through faith, and that not of yourselves; it is the gift of God, not of works, lest anyone should boast. For we are His workmanship, created in Christ

Jesus for good works, which God prepared beforehand that we should walk in them. (Ephesians 2:4-10)

The passage moves from being seated in the Heavenly places to the down-to-earth outworking of righteous good deeds here and now.

Now, therefore, you are no longer strangers and foreigners, but fellow citizens with the saints and members of the household of God, having been built on the foundation of the apostles and prophets, Jesus Christ Himself being the chief cornerstone, in whom the whole building, being joined together, grows into a holy temple in the Lord, in whom you also are being built together for a habitation of God in the Spirit. (Ephesians 2:19-22)

We all are being built together into this spiritual building where God, the Spirit, dwells. The Bible connects being a citizen of Heaven to the outworking of His righteousness in our present lives, and as a united body of believers.

Brethren, join in following my example and note those who so walk, as you have us for a pattern. For many walk, of whom I have told you often, and now tell you even weeping, that they are the enemies of the cross of Christ: whose end is destruction, whose god is their belly, and whose glory is in their shame—who set their mind on earthly things. For our citizenship is in heaven, from which we also eagerly wait for the Savior, the Lord Jesus Christ, who will transform our lowly body that it may be conformed to His glorious body, according to the working by which He is able even to subdue all things to Himself. (Philippians 3:17-21)

Heavenly citizenship is contrasted with the insanity of being an enemy of the cross and focusing on earthly things. Heavenly citizens instead expectantly look toward how they will be changed (and are being changed) to be like Christ.

If then you were raised with Christ, seek those things which are above, where Christ is, sitting at the right hand of God. Set your mind on things above, not on things on the earth. For you died, and your life is hidden with Christ in God. When Christ who is our life appears, then you also will appear with Him in glory. Therefore put to death your members which are on the earth: fornication, uncleanness, passion, evil desire, and covetousness, which is idolatry. (Colossians 3:1-5)

Again, association with Christ in the Heavenlies is the context and basis for our taking off unrighteousness and putting on Christ.

Every good gift and every perfect gift is from above, and comes down from the Father of lights, with whom there is no variation or shadow of turning. Of His own will He brought us forth by the word of truth, that we might be a kind of firstfruits of His creatures. (James 1:17-18)

We are new creations, a first fruit, a best of the crop. Our new identity is related to righteousness. We are to put off sin and put on righteousness.

But you are a chosen generation, a royal priesthood, a holy nation. His own special people, that you may proclaim the praises of Him who called you out of darkness into His marvelous light; who once were not a people but are now the people of God, who had not obtained mercy but now have obtained mercy. Beloved, I beg you as sojourners and pilgrims, abstain from fleshly lusts which war against the soul, having your conduct honorable among the Gentiles, that when they speak against you as evildoers, they may, by your good works which they observe, glorify God in the day of visitation. (I Peter 2:9-12)

Our Heavenly identity is the foundation for righteousness, which solves the sin issue. That is how simple this is. Heavenly citizenship, making us strangers and aliens to this earth, is crucial to our living out righteous lives and moving away from the struggle of sin. Our new identity gives us the freedom and foundation to embrace the grace to change. The pressure is on believers to either fit into the world or gain permission not to. Your new identity gives you permission to be different and peculiar to the glory of God.

If you were to visit Europe, ladies, would you give up bathing as often as you do now, which is more the custom there? Most Americans would resist European hygiene customs because they are foreign to us. We are of another culture. We have customs as Americans that we will continue to practice in the foreign land.

It is possible for visitors to Mexico to become so excited about the inexpensive prices that they carry as much as possible home. Many have brought back great bargains to simply find that they do not fit the decor of their American home. The bargain was not truly a bargain because the goods were useless.

Christians have permission to be different from the world because we are only visiting. We are citizens of Heaven. We do not belong here. We are not to become attached to this world's system.

We have the freedom in Christ to not live according to the rules of the world. The more you and I understand our Heavenly citizenship, the more freedom we have to say no to sin. Many tourists visit other countries without regard to whether the natives find their attire appealing. They are just visiting. What would your life be like if you truly, from the heart, embraced your Heavenly citizenship? What would bother you? What would interest you?

What would no longer really matter when compared to Heaven?

If we do not embrace our new identity, we cannot be free to say no to the world, ourselves, and sin. We are then simply trying to justify ourselves. It is a bad path that will never take us home.

Chapter 4

The New Mind

A few years ago, Jody, my wife, and I loaded a rental truck to drive from Dallas to Midland, Texas. We pulled off at a truck stop and said, "Fill her up." They did. It didn't take long for us to notice that there was a problem. We exited the highway and returned to the station. There we found out that they had put diesel fuel in a non-diesel engine. This experience parallels what is often experienced in Christianity. We have an engine that is designed to run a certain way, and we put the wrong fuel in it. It sputters and chokes and coughs, and doesn't run. Has your Christianity ever been like that? I believe the analogy is related to our Heavenly citizenship.

The problem of improper fuel can be illustrated by two individuals I knew in college. I actually knew many others with a similar tale.

The first friend we will call Davis. Davis was one of these guys who came to school, had reasonably bad behavior, but then got worse. He majored in dating, alcohol, and play. His grades weren't so hot, but he was very popular. You may have known people like him. In the course of time Davis came to the Lord and began to be transformed. We watched him change before our eyes. He learned. He grew. He changed. He became a different person. You could tell, because the gals he dated would admit that they had gone out with him to the amazement of others who would exclaim, "You went out with him?" His actions changed from bad to good.

The other example from college was involved with Young Life in high school. Let's call him Everett. He was very involved in the youth program, read his Bible, and even went on a short missionary trip. Coming out of high school, he was a leader in Christianity. But Everett began to get caught up in the proverbial college scene. He did what Davis did at first, but continued on. He dove into alcohol, and play, and all that goes with that life, all the way through college. I don't know where he is now.

Although they experienced the opposite result, I would argue that there was an identical process going on with these two young men. Both of these men put different fuels in the engine. In the course of time, you either have to change fuels or change engines. Their spiritual growth was dependent on the kind of fuel they filled their souls with.

Naturally, I must ask, "How about you?" Where are you in this process and struggle? What is going on in your Christian life? What's going on with the fuels, the engine? How well is it running? Are you hoping just to make it to the next exit? Are you thinking about creating an exit?

This chapter will look at two principles that unfailingly bring change, whether good or bad. What happened to these two men was identical as far as the process they went through. The fuels were different. There are two principles that are key to all of this. What you do with these principles, in large measure will dictate whether you sputter or whether you accelerate.

Let me begin by sharing my hope. The hope I have is the same one Paul expressed for the Colossians when he wrote his letter. He begins in chapter 1, verse 9, by saying:

For this reason we also, since the day we heard it, do not cease to pray for you, and to ask that you may be filled with the knowledge of His will in all wisdom and spiritual understanding; that you may have a walk worthy of the Lord, fully pleasing Him, being fruitful in every good work and increasing in the knowledge of God; strengthened with all might, according to

His glorious power, for all patience and long-suffering with joy. (Colossians 1:9-11)

What would it be like if we were filled with all the knowledge and all wisdom and spiritual understanding and walk worthy of the Lord, fully pleasing to Him, fruitful in every good work, increasing in the knowledge of God, strengthened with all might, according to His glorious power, with patience, longsuffering, and joy? Wow! We could be in a circus, we'd be so different than the world. That prayer is in the Bible for a reason. That prayer is a real possibility.

It makes no sense for God, through Paul, to pray it for people, to offer it for Christians, if that cannot become us. What's the relationship of this hope to Heavenly citizenship? See verses 12-14.

Giving thanks to the Father who has qualified us to be partakers of the inheritance of the saints in the light. He has delivered us from the power of darkness and translated us [or transferred us] *into the kingdom of the Son of His love, in whom we have redemption through His blood, the forgiveness of sins.* (Colossians 1:12-14)

Translated to a new kingdom! That's citizenship, new identity, and new opportunity.

We have already shown how this truth of our citizenship begins to give us permission. We all belong to Heaven; we're visiting here; we're ambassadors here; we're in a foreign country; we're just passing through; we have a purpose; we have opportunities; we have responsibilities. This is not our country. We have permission to swim against the flow, to go against the tide of culture, and to be different, because our identity is somewhere else. We don't have to fit in. If you don't understand this, it doesn't matter where you go; any culture you focus on, you will try to fit in.

A friend went away to Europe on an internship. She went away with a normal name, and she came back pronouncing her name in French! She even made us call her by the French version! Sometimes we want to fit in so badly that we change ourselves in order to do so. God's people are free to be Heavenly minded and have Heavenly behavior. We do not have to fit in.

"How do we change our life style into a Heavenly life style?" How do we make this connection between citizenship and the transformation in our walk? We can live according to joy and glorious power and strength. We can have all might and increase in the knowledge of God.

I beseech you therefore, brethren, by the mercies of God, that you present your bodies a living sacrifice, holy, acceptable to God, which is your reasonable service. And do not be conformed to this world, but be transformed by the renewing of your mind, that you may prove what is that good and acceptable and perfect will of God. (Romans 12:1-2)

You may have looked at this many times, and it's rather simple. The world is trying to conform us. "Don't let the world squeeze you into its mold" is the message here.

It is obvious that the world tries to conform us through our minds. Otherwise, why the instruction to renew it? The renewing, however, focuses on being transformed. The Greek word is *metamorphoo*. We get the word metamorphosis from the same root word. It denotes the idea of a caterpillar becoming a butterfly. That is transformation. It is also in the passive voice here, which means it is something done to us, not something we do. We do not transform ourselves. Another process acts on us. Our responsibility is to renew our mind. To renew the way we think, to change it. That's the key from our viewpoint that sets the transformation in motion.

It is not a complicated concept, and it is not unique to Romans. Colossians 2:8 reads:

Beware lest anyone cheat you through philosophy and empty deceit, according to the tradition of men, according to the basic principles

of the world, and not according to Christ.
(Colossians 2:8)

Remember the dichotomy we discussed earlier? There is the world's way and there is Christ's way. There is Heaven and there is earth. On the earthly level, some truths seem to work, but they are evil, wrong, and often destructive. This text says they cheat us, they plunder us, and they take us captive. The world's ideas come through people. It is an empty deceit. The world's philosophies seem to be intellectual and informed. Yet, there is a hook in the world's way of thinking that destroys us. It follows the tradition of men. It is tied to the principles of the world. This world's system is indeed trying to destroy believers.

It doesn't stop there, if you'll look in Colossians 2, verse 18. It says:

Let no one defraud you of your reward, taking delight in false humility and worship of angels, intruding into those things which he has not seen, vainly puffed up by his fleshly mind, not holding fast to the Head. (Colossians 2:18-19a)

The idea is that this mind set on the flesh, on the world system, is corrupted and vainly puffed up. This mindset calls things knowledge and wisdom that are visions, inflated by the mind gone amok. You need not watch television for long to see different versions of the same thing, a whirlwind of ideas that are often half fantasy and half propaganda.

It's curious to me as I study through Colossians, that there are 12 specific verses that mention our mind, or are concerned with wisdom and knowledge. Colossians includes the whole issue of the dichotomy between the truths of Heaven and the truths of the earth, and the danger the latter present. What I want to focus on though is the how-to, and I believe the how-to finds its centerpiece in chapter 3 of Colossians.

If then you were raised with Christ, seek those things which are above, where Christ is, sitting at the right hand of God. Set your mind on things above, not on the things on the earth. For you died, and your life is hidden with Christ in God. When Christ who is our life appears, then you also will appear with Him in glory. (Colossians 3:1-4)

I want to focus on the two principles of our concern. Paul says, "If then...." It carries the assumption in this context that you were raised. It also leaves room that if you're not a Christian, you were not raised with Christ. Raised with Christ carries with it the idea of identification, our identity up there with Him. The identity the context speaks of concerns those things declared about us that are associated with Him and His death, burial, and resurrection. It was ours too: our death, burial, and resurrection. These are positional truths, truths of identification, truths that have great import and impact here and now that unfortunately seem so far away that we often ignore them.

You can see in Colossians 2, verse 10, "And you are complete in Him." Same idea, a positional truth. How many of you feel complete? Do you feel like a perfect example of what a Christian is to be?

These things are declared of us. They are truths for growing up. We are complete in Christ and we are being completed in the here and now. Someday when we see Him, we will be like Him (I John 3:2). God has declared truths through which He transforms us. If you were raised with Christ, seek those things above where Christ is sitting at the right hand of God. The right hand is the place of authority where Christ is right now, waiting for His enemies to be made a footstool (Acts 2:34-35).

He is there at the right hand of the Father. He is still over all things. He has finished the salvation process as far as His death on the cross. He is there with us; we are there with Him. The text (Col. 3:2) says, "Set your mind on things above, not on things on the earth." Again, the dichotomy. It says, "For you died, and your life is hidden with Christ in God" (v. 3). The idea is that we, as to our old life and old self, have died. Our life now is hidden with Christ in God.

There's a new connection and a new life within us. "When Christ who is our life appears [the second coming], then you also will appear with Him in glory" (v. 4) because that's where we will be. We will finally come into the full expression of our citizenship.

However, what I want you to notice here are two principles. I call them the principle of disposition and the principle of focus. Consider what scholars say about this idea of seeking those things which are above and setting our mind on things above. They say there's a distinction here. I want you to get the distinction. It's the key.

Kenneth Wuest says of this passage, "The things above be constantly seeking. The word 'things', is in the emphatic position, contrasting the above things with those earthly things which the heretics were seeking after." What he means is that we have things above, Heaven; things below, earth. The heretics were seeking after worldly things. Incidentally, Wuest argues from Colossians 2:20-22 that legalism is another version of pursuing earthly things. He goes on to say about 3:2, "Set your affection" ("set your mind"—NKJV) is "To direct one's mind to a thing."[1]

Curtis Vaughn notes curiously, "The NIV interprets the commands of verses 1 and 2 as essentially the same. There may, however, be a slight difference. Setting the heart on things above (verse 1) is descriptive of the aim, the practical pursuit of the Christian life. Setting the mind (verse 2) on things above refers more to an inner disposition."[2]

Lightfoot comments, "You must not only seek heaven; you must also think heaven."[3] Vaughn adds, "There is, of course, an intimate connection between the two."

Our disposition, the way we see the world and life, is to be through Heavenly eyes. It is to be through a mindset "of Heaven." This means seeing things through the eyes of Heaven. It is looking down on our circumstances in life from that place where we are with Christ. It is a disposition. It is a perspective.

There are people that we say have an angry disposition. We mean that they have as a theme in their life, a kind of angry, irascible, irritable personality. Whatever you say to them will be taken wrong, will invite a shot back, or will stir their anger. They may be an ultimate pessimist or irritant.

We know others who have a pleasant disposition. They are nice, and they, when given lemons, make lemonade. You know the type. Whatever is dealt them in life, it seems to work out. Even if they're kind of Pollyanna-ish, they're really a lot nicer than those other people. Pleasant people are like that. We like to have them around. They have a disposition of pleasantness, of seeing things in a positive light. Therefore, whatever comes along, they see opportunity.

The point in this passage is that *we can have an earthly disposition or a Heavenly one. We can see everything in terms of the earth and how it affects us, or we can see everything in light of Heaven.* I want to offer a phrase to help you think in Heavenly terms.

Have you ever used this phrase or heard it from others? "What's in it for me?" Or, we might say to someone, "You're always thinking what's in it for you." And they respond, "So what's your point?" I want to take the "me" word out and say, *"What's in it for Heaven?"* Any decision. Any issue. Any problem. Anything you're facing in life. What if you ask the question, "What's in it for Heaven?" You may have a tragedy you're facing. You may be facing surgery, fear, or problems in a work situation, but you can still say, "What's in it for Heaven?"

The issue is perspective. Perspective affects everything. A great example is the Olympics. Those who compete are there to represent their country. If we see our athletes perform well, we know it is because they do not want to dishonor America. When they misbehave or perform poorly, we are embarrassed for our country. How much more important is Christianity and our Heavenly country? What if we thought in terms of not wanting to dishonor our country? I've heard Olympic athletes say, "I'm sorry. I let the country down today." Or, when they have won, they say, "Of course, I did it for America."

We must be disposed to thinking of Heaven as our home and the earth as only a place we are visiting. How do we change our disposition to that of Heaven? How do we gain a Heavenly disposition? We may think the concept of Heavenly citizenship is wonderful, but the process of changing our disposition must be addressed. This leads to our second principle.

How does one gain a Heavenly disposition? The answer is the principle of focus. "Seek those things which are above" (Col. 3:1). *Changing disposition occurs one truth at a time.* We focus on a truth. Study this passage, reflect on it, and you will come to the same conviction. Things above, in Heaven, represent the spiritual dimension.

Second Corinthians 4:16 (and the following verses) addresses this dichotomy between temporal things and eternal things. It speaks about things we see, earthly and temporal, and things we do not see, spiritual and Heavenly. Specifically, it calls us to focus our eyes of faith on spiritual things in order to be transformed. *When we focus our mind on a spiritual truth, we must focus on one truth at a time in order to transform the whole disposition.*

This principle of focus is likened to the bricks in a wall. The disposition is the wall, or the building. The focus is the single brick. How do you build a wall? One brick at a time. If we want a godly disposition, but don't get into the process of focusing on each truth; on specific things we learn and understand about our identity in the Lord and our citizenship in Heaven; how this spiritual life works and how to walk in the Spirit; and even the importance of transformation by truth, we will not change. We must focus on one truth at a time. This is the process that transforms our disposition. Have you made the mistake of trying to focus on too many truths at once, knowing more but changing little?

There is also another side to this process of focus. Disposition selects a certain focus. In other words, there's a cycle here where each truth will begin to support or reinforce another. If you are building a brick wall, and you have completed a good portion of the wall, it has a certain pattern to it and a certain flavor of the brick. When you reach out and take a brick that does not match, you throw it away.

The New Mind

When our disposition is earthly, we tend to throw away spiritual truths because they don't match our disposition. When we gain a Heavenly disposition, we throw away the earthly truths, because they don't match either. The process reinforces itself. This is partly of why change is so hard.

It's the same with matching the decor in a room. When you bring in something that doesn't match at all, it is thrown out. If we placed bright, canary yellow chairs in a traditional church auditorium, they would seem out of place. If a church had an orange vinyl pew covering, like that in fast food restaurants, worshipers would not feel invited to stay long and make themselves at home. Each individual piece must match the pattern of the whole.

We are born with a disposition toward earthly things. We are inbred with a love of the world. Yet, we become citizens of Heaven when we are born again, and are given the capacity for a new disposition. The old disposition needs to be changed to the new one. But change is difficult. There's another version of these principles in the Word of God: the laws of sowing and reaping. We will all reap as we sow. If you sow to the flesh, you'll reap from the flesh. If you sow to the Spirit, you'll reap from the Spirit. The curious thing about these laws is that they are not particular. They are effective in either a bad direction or a good one.

When we are in an earthly cycle, we are focused on things on the earth. We get caught up in what we do. We are concerned about the day-to-day affairs of life and they reinforce the "truths of this world, and the world's ways of living this life."

When we become citizens of Heaven and begin to move in a Heavenly cycle, there is no way for the world's philosophies to take root, because they do not match the pattern of our disposition. We then cast aside the world's philosophies and look for truths that compliment the Heavenly pattern of our lives.

If we are disposed toward earth, we feel more like a citizen of earth, and think that this earth is all that counts. We begin to buy the lies of the earth because they seem to make sense. We may think, "You only go around once," or "Don't I deserve a little pleasure, a little fun?"

If you have a disposition that's earthly, then the way you see money and interact with money will corrupt you. How do you handle your time? Is it reinforcing healthy friendships or dangerous ones?

If you surround yourself with people who do not share your opinion of Christianity and of Heavenly citizenship, remember that those people will not be talking the truths you need to change your disposition. I'm not suggesting that you should not have unbelieving friends, only that your most intimate friends should be believers. If they are unbelievers, they will be playing into unraveling this Heaven-sent opportunity to know all wisdom, fruit, good work, the knowledge of God, and your being strengthened with all might.

How you interact with your children, the way you see them, the way you see work, the way you see your spouse, even things like travel plans, are all impacted by your disposition and your efforts to change one truth at a time. Often, we are simply seeking some kind of an escape and relief, or we are trying to cope the way the world wants us to cope.

What would happen if you began to ask, "What's in it for Heaven?" Okay, I'm going on a trip. "What's in it for Heaven?" How does it relate there? How about my money? "What's in it for Heaven?" How about my time and the way I manage it? "What's in it for Heaven?" Do you see the difference? The disposition of Heaven offers a way to make every aspect of your life match the pattern of being a citizen of Heaven. How about friends? "What's in it for Heaven?" My children? "What's in it for Heaven?" My work? "What's in it for Heaven?" My wife or my husband? "What's in it for Heaven?" School? "What's in it for Heaven?"

Everything you do comes back to a Heavenly disposition and it is developed by focusing on one truth at a time. Essentially what happened to Davis and to Everett was that very thing. Davis began to focus on truths in the Word of God that were spiritual. They gave him a new disposition, a new way to think about life, and he grew up in the Savior. Everett, on the other hand, began to give priority to worldly things that had no relationship to Heaven, no way to get them related to Heaven, and they unraveled his spiritual life and his spiritual walk, and brought him down. How about you?

The answer is simple. Focus on truths, a brick at a time, to embrace a Heavenly perspective that befits a citizen of Heaven.

Chapter 5

The Protection
of Heaven

I have always been intrigued with fire. Once, a friend and I started a fire in the woods near our house. My friend, Steve, was about six and I was four or five. We played in the woods near school. One day Steve pulled out a pack of matches and wanted to start a fire. He had me hold the leaf while he lit the match. I held the leaf as long as I could, but soon dropped it. This caught the other leaves on fire, which caught the woods on fire.

We went home and commenced to lie to Mother. We blamed it on some boys that we claimed were chasing us. Of course, we smelled like smoke. The correction I received will not be forgotten. I had to wait for Dad to come home to whip me, and then was confined to my yard for a week. This was one of my first introductions to the concept of peer pressure. Even as a four or five-year-old, I knew that we should not have been playing with matches. Yet, I yielded.

When I was involved with Campus Crusade for Christ at the University of Alabama, I led evangelism the last year in school. We decided to do a survey. Sometimes surveys have been a come-on to share the gospel. I didn't like that idea. I wanted to actually do something with the survey that would be useful. We made a commitment to take the survey among the leaders of the University of Alabama, promising to publish the results in the school newspaper. One question was, "What is the greatest problem facing college students?" We were thinking they would answer drugs, finances, homework, scheduling, or problems at home. However, the overwhelming response among the leaders of the student body at the University of Alabama that year was peer pressure.

It strikes me that if people were saying that peer pressure is a great problem in college, then they feel constrained to do things they don't want to. That is the nature of peer pressure.

Have you ever struggled with peer pressure? I'd like to suggest that not only have you struggled, but you do struggle. A little volume I have enjoyed down through the years is called *The Human Connection: How People Change People*. There are a couple of relevant experiments mentioned by the authors, Bolt and Myers. "In one of the segments of the television program 'Candid Camera,' an unsuspecting person waits in an office building for an elevator. The elevator arrives, the doors open, and the passenger steps in. One by one others follow, but then proceed to behave strangely. They all face the back. The victim peers quizzically at each, fidgets nervously and then meekly conforms."[1]

The second experiment also demonstrates the power of peer influence.

Imagine that you have volunteered to participate in an experiment on a visual judgment. You and seven other participants are seated in front of two cards on which are lines of varying lengths. Your task is to judge which of three lines is closest in length to a fourth line, which serves as the standard. It is clear to you that line B is the correct answer. But the first person to make a judgment looks carefully at the lines and says 'Line A.' To your surprise so does the second and the third and so on down the line. When your turn finally comes, what will you say? Will you agree with the majority or will you exercise critical judgment and state what you believe is right?

Asked to predict their own reaction, most people say they will resist influence and report what they know is right...only a quarter, however, of the subjects were able to resist the false norms consistently. [2]

Isn't this hard to fathom? Only one in four would not yield to the other six.

The authors ask:

To what degree can social pressure lead us to violate our moral standards? Is it possible that someone can induce us to engage in harmful, destructive acts? Milgram tried to answer this question in what have become the most famous studies in social psychology. As mentioned in chapter 2 [Bolt and Myers] men from diverse backgrounds and occupations were recruited to participate in an experiment said to investigate the effects of punishment on learning. The participants were assigned the role of teacher. His task was to deliver an electric shock to the "student" whenever a mistake was made on a simple learning task. The switches on the shock generator ranged from a mild 15 volts to a supposedly dangerous 450 volts. The experimenter instructed the teacher to begin punishment of initial errors with the mild shock and to raise the voltage each time an additional error was made until the highest voltage was being administered. The "student" was an accomplice of the experimenter who, although he received no shock, had been carefully coached to act as though he did. When the student made many mistakes and loudly protested the shocks, the experimenter told the teacher to continue raising the voltage. How far did subjects go? When Milgram described the experiment to some psychiatrists, college students and middle class adults, virtually no one expected anyone to proceed to the end. The psychiatrists guessed one in a thousand. Contrary to the expectation, almost two-thirds of the participants fully obeyed delivering the greatest possible shock.

How could subjects bring themselves to continue shocking the victim? Were they evil people? No. They were not unusually hostile or vicious. Many belonged to Christian churches and when asked, firmly stated their moral opposition to injuring others.[3]

It is a part of our nature as humans to conform to the majority. Have you ever considered peer pressure in the areas of time, money, and people? What I mean by that is, are you guided and directed by the social forces and pressures around you? How about where you spend your money? What sorts of things do you purchase in terms of homes, cars, appliances, toys, games, and travel? What people do you spend time with? To what degree are your actions and relationships guided by social peer pressure, simply because those things are expected and anticipated in the culture?

We understand that Heavenly citizenship means that we, as believers, are citizens of Heaven. We are only visiting here. We are aliens and strangers. We are going to Heaven someday. We are on earth for a reason. In the last chapter we will look at how this fact relates to impacting the world. We will discuss the idea of social activism as opposed to fulfilling the Great Commission. J. Vernon McGee is noted for saying, "We don't want to make the world a better place to go to hell in. God has called us to go fishing, not clean up the pond."

In this chapter we're going to look at how Heavenly citizenship relates to protecting us from the world. *If we are not protected from the world, it's going to be very difficult to impact it.* I'll remind you of a passage from Matthew 5 where Christ says:

You are the salt of the earth; but if the salt loses its flavor, how shall it be seasoned? It is then good for nothing but to be thrown out and trampled under foot by men. You are the light of the world. A city that is set on a hill cannot be hidden. Nor do they light a lamp and put it under a basket, but on a lampstand, and it gives light to all who are in the house. Let your light so shine before men, that they may see your good works and glorify your Father in heaven. (Matthew 5:13-16)

We are to be salty. We are to be light. Ephesians, Titus, and First Peter especially emphasize this principle. The focus in all these books is our different lives before the world, not efforts on our part to conform the world to our standards. They will see our differentness and "glorify the Father," not see it and follow our moral example. Our different lives may attract them to God, but our deeds will never change the heart of an evil world. We are to be different in a way that is un-impacted by the world, but rather impacts the world.

Peer pressure, conforming to the world, is what we need protection from. You may not have thought about it, but Heavenly citizenship is one of the chief elements of protection for you. We're going to look simply at the problem and the answer.

Hudson Taylor founded the China Inland Mission many years ago. He did something rather radical in those days when he went to China. Mission organizations were concerned about converting people to Christianity, but they had unfortunately confused Christianity with the British culture. Hudson Taylor did something unique and strange. He put on Chinese clothing, grew a beard, and did what he could to relate to the Chinese.

What Taylor did was radical, though most missions follow his pattern today. Missionaries try to understand the culture, relate to it, and belong to it. Then they bring the message of the grace of God without trying to change the culture to match their own. God will affect change in the culture as they learn the Word of God and apply it.

The principle is brilliant; but it is also, unfortunately, dangerous. When it turns around and moves to the internal sinful tendency to conform to the world, then we are adapting and becoming like them, not for the purpose of communicating a message, but, for the purpose of fitting in. It then becomes dangerous.

Most people in the world are citizens of the earth. The earth is all they have. As citizens of earth, they belong to the global village—the community of earth, as well as their locality. There is a desire, as a citizen of earth, to fit into this community and belong. In order to do that you've got to do what everybody else is doing. The world system encourages conformity to the standard.

There are three options immigrants have when they come into this country. If they intend to stay, they normally like to fit in. My grandmother taught English to a Laotian boy who came to America some years ago. This boy wanted to belong to America and be an American. As a result, he wanted to become a Christian. He thought Christianity was the religion for America. Therefore, if he would embrace that religion, it allowed him to conform all the more. He may have truly come to Christ. I have no idea. However, the initial motivation was his deepest desire to belong and fit in.

Immigrants often have their children speak English. They will not try to force their language on a culture; they will do everything they can to fit in and belong because they want to be Americans.

There's a second option for an immigrant. If they do not intend to stay, they will not particularly try to fit in. They will try to endure and get along. We see a similar phenomenon with many who attend a church briefly. We have couples who have been told they're going to be moved by the company in four months. It is very hard to belong if you think you are temporary. That's the nature of an immigrant who comes but does not intend to stay. They will visit. They will keep their customs, then leave.

The third option for an immigrant is to live within an isolated sub-culture within the larger community. A most graphic example in America is Chinatown. They have a community that is somewhat Americanized, yet you can find a great Chinese culture that may become further developed than that in their original country. We see this with Italian communities and Jewish communities and we could list all kinds of ethnic groups. They come to a country but don't entirely belong to it because they maintain their own community and identity.

Often these folks remain separate because they do not want to lose their culture. Although they want the benefits of the larger society, they do not want to conform in every way.

We will yield to those people we are around. In First Corinthians 15:33 it says, "Evil company corrupts good habits [morals]." It is the nature of the beast. This is addressed by the apostle Peter.

First Peter 1:1 says: "Peter, an apostle of Jesus Christ, To the pilgrims of the Dispersion...."

Peter is addressing them as pilgrims, as aliens. He wrote the pilgrims of the dispersion in Pontus, Galatia, Cappadocia, Asia, and Bithynia. They were scattered, they were believers, and they were pilgrims.

Notice First Peter 1:18:

Knowing that you were not redeemed with corruptible things, like silver or gold, from your aimless conduct received by tradition from your fathers. (I Peter 1:18)

Peter is alluding to the very fact we are considering about the world, the earthly citizenship, and the earthly community. He calls what they received from tradition aimless. Citizens of earth who focus on the earth are living an aimless existence. Peter doesn't stop there.

First Peter 2:9 reads:

But you are a chosen generation, a royal priesthood, a holy nation [here's that Heavenly citizenship theme], *His own special people, that you may proclaim the praises of Him who called you out of darkness into His marvelous light.* (I Peter 2:9)

Darkness represents the earth; that earthly region, earthly citizenship.

Therefore, since Christ suffered for us in the flesh, arm yourselves also with the same mind, for he who has suffered in the flesh has ceased from sin, that he no longer should live the rest of his time in the flesh for the lusts of men [conformity], *but for the will of God. For we have spent enough of our past lifetime in doing the will of the Gentiles—when we walked in licentiousness, lusts, drunkenness, revelries, drinking parties, and abominable idolatries. In regard to these, they think it strange that you do not run with them in the same flood of dissipation, speaking evil of you.* (I Peter 4:1-4)

Those in the world will speak evil of you when you say no to them because you are not conforming to the world. You are not conforming to the citizenship of the earth and its darkness and aimlessness. Worldliness and peer pressure in effect are the same thing. It is what Paul speaks of in Romans 12:2 when he warns of the world trying to squeeze you into its mold. There is a constant pressure on us as Christians, as citizens of Heaven, to be formed and shaped like the world wants us to be. If we're not protected from that conformity, then we will have no saltiness, we will have no light, we will have no savor, and we will be effectively worthless. Our lives will "taste" no different than the world.

There is no guarantee in the Word of God that you are going to grow spiritually. Ultimately you will be conformed to the image of Christ (Rom. 8:28-29), but misunderstanding this truth will teach you that "pride comes before a fall." I want you to understand that what I'm sharing with you is vital to protect you from being swallowed up by the world. I don't care who you are, how old, how young, or how mature, you can be swallowed by the world; but you will not be if you follow the answer.

The answer is simply this, living as citizens of Heaven in a gathered community. The answer is the same dynamic in peer pressure, only used for good. It is Heavenly citizenship in a gathered community of citizens. Renewal of the mind, walking in Christ, walking in righteousness; all these things relate, but conceptually this is the bigger idea, the context for protection. There are two keys to overcoming worldly peer pressure as citizens of Heaven.

First, citizenship in Heaven gives permission to not conform. When we understand that we are citizens of Heaven, we belong to another country, and we are temporarily here, then we are free not to embrace this country of earth. We are looking and longing for that Heavenly home someday. We are here as representatives. We have a new set of privileges, a new set of protections, and a new set of opportunities in our calling as citizens. We, therefore, have permission to not yield to the way the world says do it. We gain permission as a citizen of Heaven to say no to the world.

The second key regards being a part of a gathered community. The local church gives us support to not conform. Did you hear that? *Citizenship in Heaven gives us permission to not conform. A gathered community gives us support to not conform.* Even though we are citizens of Heaven and have permission, if we do not find a supportive community of fellow citizens, we are going to have a hard time beating back the world on our own. Remember, there can be no Lone Ranger Christians.

It is this combination between citizenship and a gathered community of other citizens that supports, feeds, and fits us with these people with whom we associate, reminding us we are citizens, helping us say no to the world, no to self, yes to the Lord and His purposes, and yes to one another. This is a shared community.

The reason a teen does not yield to peer pressure is simply this: Your family has two things going for it. One is that your parents have values and they have tried to communicate them to you. The second is that you have at least an equal if not better concern and relationship with your family than you do with what's going on in school and the culture.

What happens with peer pressure is simple. The pressure in the world is greater than the pressure in the family system. When a family is close, they know each other, they are communicating, and they're loving each other. Then most kids do not want to embarrass, hurt, and frustrate mom and dad. They have a relationship and they love them. For the most part, they are very thankful that there is someone who gives them an excuse to say no. They don't want to say yes. When a family is close, then there is a basis for pressure to be resisted.

When we allow our kids to drift off, and the relationships they have with friends and those in the world exceed the relationships in the family and in the church, then they are ill-equipped to do anything except yield to whatever is going on out there.

But you are a chosen generation, a royal priesthood, a holy nation, His own special people, that you may proclaim the praises of Him who called you out of darkness into His marvelous light; who once were not a people but are now the people of God, who had not obtained mercy but now have obtained mercy. Beloved [those who know Christ, those who are citizens of Heaven], *I beg you as sojourners and pilgrims, abstain from fleshly lusts which war against*

*the soul, having your conduct honorable among
the Gentiles, that when they speak against you
as evildoers, they may, by your good works
which they observe, glorify God in the day of
visitation.* (I Peter 2:9-12)

The issue of citizenship and conformity to the
world is intimately connected with remembering
that you are a sojourner and a pilgrim on this earth.
We are only here for a time on our way to a better
country.

Peter also includes the aspect of community found
in the local church as an important part of our non-
conformity to peer pressure. First Peter 4:8a says,
"And above all things have fervent love for one
another." If you are going to love one another, and
it involves Christians, you are going to have to be
together. Peter continued, "Be hospitable to one another without grumbling. As each one has received a
gift, minister it to one another..." (vv. 9-10). You
can't use a spiritual gift if there are no others
around. This is one of the reasons the gift of ton-
gues, even if you believe it's for today, should not be
used in private. It should be used for the Body.
Gifts are not given to be used on oneself. They are
given to edify others. Verse 10 continues, "...to one
another as good stewards of the manifold grace of
God." According to Peter, being a good steward of
God's grace means using our gifts for one another's
benefit in a gathered community, a local church.

But let none of you suffer as a murderer, a thief, an evildoer, or as a busybody in other people's matters. Yet if anyone suffers as a Christian, let him not be ashamed, but let him glorify God in this matter. For the time has come for judgment to begin at the house of God; and if it begins with us first, what will be the end of those who do not obey the gospel of God? (I Peter 4:15-17)

The house of God is certainly a broad concept in this epistle. However, you cannot talk about the church around the world except in terms of local churches, local expressions, and local communities. You can have all the understanding of the Word of God and think you are a part of the Church, but if you sit in your apartment or your house alone all the time and call that Christianity, you will never experience what God intended Christianity to be. In fact, you will likely drift further from the Lord.

First Peter 5:2 says, "Shepherd the flock of God which is among you ["among you" refers to a local Church], serving as overseers, not by constraint but willingly, not for dishonest gain but eagerly; nor as being lords over those entrusted to you, but being examples to the flock." He is exhorting the local group, the local assembly, and the local concern. "Likewise you younger people, submit yourselves to your elders. Yes, all of you be submissive to one another..." (v. 5). How can we submit to one another if we are not together? We can't.

It is our citizenship in Heaven that gives us permission to not conform, but it is being in a gathered community that gives us the support to not conform.

We want to impact and touch this world. We do not want to be impacted by it. What sense does it make to find who we are in the earth and her toys and her trinkets? It makes no sense. What sense is it to make your gathered community or support with those of the earth and those who are citizens of the earth? None whatsoever.

We can't love people we don't spend time with. We can't be loved by people we don't spend time with. We certainly can't be protected. Bolt and Myers also add this thought:

> If people are to live distinctively Christian lives, the spirit of individualism must be overcome. Loyalty to Christ is next to impossible without a relationship to his body, to a fellowship of Christians who contribute to each other's upbuilding. Although time and again we are reminded that the New Testament church was a believing community, we have lost this perspective...Arthur Gish puts it more strongly, "The church should not accept confessions of faith and commitments without providing nurture and support to help people keep their promises. We fail

people by not supporting and helping them keep their commitments."[4]

What is peer pressure doing to you? How is the world forcing you to live contrary to Christ? How is the world watering down your faith? Are the areas of struggle in your life explained, at least in part, by your focus on fitting into the world and being at a distance from a loving church community?

Those of us who understand our citizenship, our need for community, and are involved, know what I'm talking about. Is there room in your heart and time schedule for another fellow citizen? There needs to be room because that's what authentic Christianity is about and it provides protection for you. God never intended for us to go it alone. If you have no church, find one. The Spirit of God is alive among true believers. If you are involved in something Christ-centered that is not the Church, that is good, but it is still less than God's best. Find a community of pilgrims and love them with all your heart.

Chapter 6

The Plan of Heaven
Part I: Expanding
the Empire

Like most Christians, my experiences with evangelism are varied. I will never forget my first attempt when I was in the eighth grade. I don't believe I was actually a Christian at the time but I had been reading the parables in *Good News for Modern Man*. Another young man and I got into an altercation about something at the lockers. I don't remember which parable I had read, but I looked at him and said, "I love you." He hit me in the face. I promise you, right in the eye. I turned the other cheek and then beat him out of his position on the football team.

My second experience with evangelism was also negative. I asked a friend with Campus Crusade for

Christ about witnessing. He said, "Great, here's how you do it." He took me to dormitories, knocking on doors, waking guys up and talking to them about Christ. It was weird. I mean it was just strange. I tolerated it and survived.

One of the more positive experiences I remember was a gal that I fell in love with for a couple of weeks one summer, in ninth grade at a summer conference. Her name was Katy. Katy shared with me all about the return of Christ and I was fascinated. I had never heard about prophecy. All I remember from our conversations was, "Don't trust any Jesus that doesn't come in the air." That's all I remember. Antichrist, I got this straight. If he's not in the air, wrong one. She was not attacking me; she was sharing beliefs she was interested in. It was intriguing and drawing.

Later, I tried to evangelize a close personal friend. He was older and a role model. I was headed to a college summer project and decided that I needed to witness to all the individuals I was close to before I went. I felt hypocritical to participate in beach evangelism without having spoken to friends and family. I went to this individual and I systematically went through every argument he had against Christianity because I knew him so well. I nailed every argument. This person finally looked at me and said to the last argument, "Well, you got me there; but you can't make me believe." I committed a crime. I pushed, found fault, and attacked. I won the argument, but not the soul.

Most believers see evangelism as something negative. We look at confronting others as fearful and demeaning. Our methods have often sent people farther from God, rather than drawing them nearer to Him. Evangelism has often become a guilt-ridden exercise that we participate in only grudgingly, if at all. Yet, evangelism is the centerpiece of the plan of Heaven. It is how the Empire of Heaven is expanded, which in turn is God's plan for the earth in our age.

Why do we have such a problem with evangelism? Why would we rather be doing something else than even talking about evangelism? I taught a series on evangelism a few years ago from the pulpit. We watched the attendance nosedive. Why would bringing up a topic that is so important, about a message that is so vital, create this response? I have a couple of suggestions.

The first is that we're consumed with being earthly citizens. We are emotionally trapped as citizens of the earth. There are four things I believe affect us as earthly citizens.

The first is this: In America we have a priority on private opinion. Private opinion equals truth in America. That's why television and radio talk shows are so popular. We're all just sharing our opinion... as though it means something. Unfortunately, it does in America because personal opinion is authoritative. There are social dynamics involved.

Think about our society's view of evangelism. Some would claim we are taking our private opinion and trying to force it on another person's private opinion. That is simply against our culture's rules. America is increasingly individualistic and relativistic. Anyone who believes in an absolute is attacked. We idolize the notion that no one can impose an idea on another.

The second negative influence of an earthly focus is the separation of church and state. This has come to be understood as a complete separation. The only place for religious talk is church, according to this concept. Many in our culture would say that, when you step out of your church building, you're in the realm of forcing your religion on everyone else.

The third earthly concept that affects our view of evangelism is something called pluralism. In our country the idea that there is such great diverse mixing of ethnic groups, orientations, and perspectives is held in high regard. It's a plural country. America is a melting pot, mixing cultures that do not blend together easily. As a result, different people have different customs, different ways of doing things, and different ways of understanding things. Our politically correct response is to appreciate it.

The fourth influence is the history of evangelism in America. The history of evangelism, particularly the aggressive nature of much of the evangelism in the last 30 or 40 years, has conditioned us to have a negative attitude toward trying to reach others for Christ.

Finally, these elements of an earthly entanglement converge to create a flawed and damaging view of evangelism. Evangelism in our day feels like taking someone's lower jaw in one hand and taking the gospel in the other and just shoving it down his throat. I remember that the mentality among a few of my friends in college was if you couldn't get it shoved down their throat, you'd rationalize, "Well, they're blind. No hope for them. I did what I could."

These notions in our society do not encourage us to share the gospel. There was a time in America, and in other societies, when people were open to the interaction of ideas. New things were acceptable, and anything could be discussed within reason. These days, however, you can't interact and talk about anything because it is considered forcing one's opinion or religion on another.

The second reason we struggle with evangelism is that we have not properly defined it. Our definition of evangelism is unbiblical, with the unbiblical fruit of keeping God's good news for mankind to ourselves. Our definitions affect our understanding and interactions in life. Let me offer a couple of examples.

The nature of a job description is that it should be an agreement about the responsibilities of a particular position. If you have ever accepted a job and the responsibilities were different than the description, you felt betrayed, irritated, and frustrated. The company had a different definition of your position than you did.

Definitions, if they are unknown, can be frightening. As a child, my friends used to say things like, "Oh! You have garments all over you." Often children cried about this because they didn't know the definition. Or, "Oh! Your epidermis is showing!" Epidermis is your skin. Garments are clothes. The way we define things will affect us, especially when we must guess at a definition of something we don't understand.

The world has convinced most Christians that "evangelism is telling someone who doesn't want to know, something he doesn't want to hear—all at the risk of rejection and offense." That's what many think evangelism is—telling the gospel to someone who cares nothing about it, and forcing it on them, with the result of offending them and being rejected, or having to reject them yourself.

What's the solution? Heavenly citizenship! Heavenly citizenship gives us a new and proper definition, along with overcoming the objections of the world. The nature of Heavenly citizenship and the nature of the passage we'll look at will give us a new way to think about evangelism. When we change our definition, we'll change our life.

Second Corinthians 5:18 begins,

Now all things are of God, who has reconciled us to Himself through Jesus Christ, and has given us the ministry of reconciliation, that is, that God was in Christ reconciling the world to Himself, not imputing their trespasses to them, and has committed to us the word of reconciliation. Therefore we are ambassadors for Christ, as though God were pleading through us: we implore you on Christ's behalf, be reconciled to God. (II Corinthians 5:18-20)

This passage is not complicated. My goal is to slow down and get you to read something carefully and think about it. There are three simple points. The first is that God has reconciled us to Himself. The second is that God has reconciled us through Jesus Christ. The third is that God has given us the ministry of reconciliation.

God has reconciled us to Himself. "Now all things are of God." That phrase specifically looks to the context of the things. It's not necessary that everything is of God, though in a sense it is. The things Paul is referring to are within the context of being a new creation in Christ, the motivation of love, of reaching out to others, denying oneself, and a number of themes throughout the book. These things are of God who has reconciled us to Himself.

Reconciliation is a concept that's not complicated. All it means is you've taken two that are opposed and disagree and made them agree. You made them friends. You take former enemies and make them friends. We use the word commonly in reconciling a bank statement. When you have a balance from the bank and another in the checkbook, you figure out where the error is so that they are reconciled, or in agreement.

God has reconciled us to Himself. We were, at one point, enemies of God. At one point, we were friends in Adam. In his fall, we inherited enemy status toward God and received a nature of sin. We further became confirmed enemies by sinning for ourselves. It could have been active or it could have been passive, but we were enemies in our hearts. We were enemies in our actions to the living God. The text says that "He has reconciled us."

Christianity is about a holy God figuring out how to bring unholy mankind into harmony and friendship, to end the rebellion and our status as enemies.

> *And you, who once were alienated and enemies in your mind by wicked works, yet now He has reconciled in the body of His flesh through death, to present you holy, and blameless, and irreproachable in His sight.* (Colossians 1:21-22)

He is holy and righteous. Reconciliation means that He must figure out a way to make us holy and righteous in order to have a relationship with Him.

> *For if when we were enemies we were reconciled to God through the death of His Son, much more, having been reconciled, we shall be saved by His life.* (Romans 5:10)

Again we see the idea that we have an enemy issue with the living God and He has reconciled us. He not only initiates the process, but He sees it through. I'm often surprised at how much credit we try to take in reconciliation, when apart from God the idea would have never occurred to us. This leads us to the second point.

God reconciled us through Jesus Christ. Computer programs for reconciling figures often have a feature which forces the figures to agree. That means, if the balance in your checkbook doesn't add up to the one in the bank, it doesn't matter. You can enter this command and it will force agreement. Some people have the idea that if they'll just believe in God, or do what they can, or be good, it is like punching that forced balance agreement command. "God can't be too upset with me. I'm a pretty good fellow. I'm no Hitler." The problem is that God designed a very specific way to reconcile us. He took the initiative and it was through Christ.

Jesus Christ came to earth, both as a man and as God, to pay a debt that we could only pay with our lives forever. God is holy. He was offended and is offended by our sin. The sin issue must be dealt with. God came up with a creative option to send an eternal being to pay an eternal debt to an eternal God. He poured His wrath on Christ; He took our sin off of us and put it on Him. He took His righteousness off Him and put it on us. He declared it so. He said it to be true. It worked in the dynamics within the Godhead and the dynamics within us as humans. "For He made Him who knew no sin to be sin for us, that we might become the righteousness of God in Him" (II Cor. 5:21).

Jesus Christ died on the cross for you. You've probably heard this for years. Many times we don't understand it because we don't understand first that we are enemies, and second that we are sinners and we need our sin removed. God provided through Christ. He took all of our sin and put it on Him so that we could stand before a holy God, declared righteous, through the death of His Son. He was a substitute.

Robert McGee offers us a practical clarification from his counseling experience.

> God's solution to the fear of rejection is based on Christ's sacrificial payment of our sins. Through this payment, we find forgiveness, reconciliation, and total acceptance through Christ. Reconciliation means that those who were enemies have become friends.

> ...As I talked with Pam, it became obvious that she did not understand this great truth of reconciliation. Three years into her marriage, Pam had committed adultery with a man at her office. The guilt that plagued her made it hard for her to feel acceptable to God. Her guilt persisted even though she had confessed her sin to God and to her husband. And both had forgiven her. Four years after the affair, she still could not forgive herself for what she had done.

> Finally as we talked, I became frustrated with her reluctance to believe that she was forgiven by God. I told her, "But to hear you tell it, one would think God could never forgive you of a sin like that."

> "That's right," she replied. "I don't think He ever will."

> "But God doesn't base His love and acceptance of us on our performance," I stated. "If

ever there is a sin so filthy and vile that makes us less acceptable to Him, then the cross is insufficient. If the cross isn't sufficient for any particular sin, then the Bible is in error when it says that He forgave all your sins" (Colossians 2:13-15). God took our sins and cancelled them by nailing them to Christ's cross. In this way God also took away Satan's power to condemn us for sin. So you see, nothing you will ever do can nullify your reconciliation and make you unacceptable to God.

All of us need to realize the truth I was trying to communicate to Pam. Salvation is not simply a ticket to heaven. It is the beginning of a dynamic new relationship with God. Justification is the doctrine that explains the judicial facts of our forgiveness and righteousness in Christ. Reconciliation explains the relational aspect of our salvation. The moment we receive Christ by faith, we enter into a personal relationship with Him. We are united with God in an eternal and inseparable bond (Romans 8:38,39). We are bound in an indissoluble union with Him, as a joint-heir with Christ. The Holy Spirit has sealed us in that relationship, and we are absolutely secure in Christ.[1]

As those who are reconciled to God, He has given to us the ministry of reconciliation. Second Corinthians 5:18 reads, "...given us the ministry of reconciliation."

Again in verse 20 it says, "Therefore we are ambassadors for Christ, as though God were pleading through us: we implore you on Christ's behalf, be reconciled to God." This reconciliation with God is objective, which means it's positionally true; and it is subjective, which means we experience it. Though we're reconciled to God we are being reconciled to God. We are in a process of sorting it out and growing closer and enjoying that reconciliation. We are complete in Christ and we are being completed on the earth. Someday we'll be like him when we see Him (I John 3:2).

All those who are in Christ are His ambassadors. An ambassador represents one nation to another. He or she is often respected, but not necessarily. Sometimes they are in danger of being killed, sometimes in danger at the embassy, to which the local church might be compared. The goal is to fairly and appropriately represent the country, oftentimes with an eye toward reconciling or improving the relationship between the countries.

If you are a citizen of Heaven, rather than allowing the world to squeeze you into a mold, and rather than belonging to the culture, you, as an ambassador, are in a position to represent the government you serve—Heaven. It doesn't matter what your view of the political situation is. Are you fairly representing information to the country you're in from the country you truly belong to? We are foreigners here for only a limited time.

We don't have to play the games of the culture. We are here to represent the living God, His government, and His country. Our hearts long for the new nation, with a future—Heaven.

The nature of this ambassador's commission is found in verse 20, "Therefore we are ambassadors for Christ, as though God were pleading through us: we implore you on Christ's behalf, be reconciled to God." *We are not here to jump down people's throats, but to simply invite them to be reconciled to God, to become friends with Him again, and to give up the enemy relationship.* That's all it is. This is the correct definition of evangelism.

Evangelism is not a dramatic struggle. It is not finding the perfect technique. It doesn't even have to be offensive. It is an issue of just freely offering the fact that God wants to be reconciled and He has provided for it through His Son. "Please be reconciled." The passage here says, "Pleading through." We can't make people believe. We can't force the gospel on them, but we can offer it. We can offer it without offense. As Dr. Howard Hendricks has observed, "Most of us don't suffer for righteousness' sake, but for stupidity's sake." Much of our evangelism, or lack thereof, is due to stupidity born from a wayward definition.

The definition of evangelism should read, "*Evangelism: as an ambassador and without offense, pleading with those estranged from God to be reconciled to*

Him who took the initiative by sending His Son, Jesus Christ." That's what evangelism is. We're not calling people to become "chummy" with the God of creation, but we are inviting them to enter into a Heavenly friendship with Him.

A conference speaker once shared this story from his busy life and travels. He was riding in a jet one day and someone asked him, "What do you do?" He said, "Well, I'm an ambassador." "An ambassador? What country?" He responds, "It's bigger than a country!" The listener said, "What coalition of nations?" "Oh, it's bigger than a coalition of nations!" "Then what do you represent?" "A kingdom, an empire," the speaker said. "What is it?" "It's the kingdom of God. The empire of Christ." Now that's biblical thinking.

My concern here is to ask and answer the question, "How do we expand this empire?" The way we expand it is by walking with Christ and serving as ambassadors from Heaven to invite those people who long to be reconciled to God, to be reconciled. We expand the empire by being about the same old things Christians have done for centuries, which is without offense, walking in love, and inviting people to be reconciled through Christ. We are free to do that when we understand that we are citizens of Heaven who are commissioned as Heaven's ambassadors. God deputized all of us who know Christ as ambassadors of this goodwill of the grace of God. Remember, reconciliation is for Christians too. Expanding the empire involves building one another up in Christ.

As we take fellow citizens who have strayed from the Lord and bring them back, then we increase the number of available ambassadors. The only limitation to this approach to expanding the empire is that it requires faith. It requires a heart that believes if we share the message He will take care of the results. It isn't much of a method and would hardly make a training program. Nonetheless, it is the strategy He has always returned us to and used from the beginning. It's the plan of Heaven. May He use it again, through you.

Chapter 7

The Plan of Heaven Part II: Heaven vs. Politics

Few of us would know what to do if an expectant mother were to go into labor in our living room. Perhaps we would have the strength to simply take each part of the delivery one step at a time and seek help from an experienced professional. Perhaps we would panic and have to be sent out of the room to boil water. At times, I am afraid that the Church falls into panic instead of looking to God one step at a time.

Christian America is greatly off track these days, and the consequences are eternal. My call here is to return to God's Word by shedding a doomed and carnal strategy to save the nation. God has a strategy.

It is time to return to His plan as citizens of Heaven. So much of Christianity has acted like a panicking friend who is told to "boil water" instead of helping deliver the baby—noisy and in the way! It isn't too late, we can return to God and His strategy.

Let's begin by considering America. We are facing epidemics such as AIDS. We are facing riots in cities. We are facing economic uncertainty which some label "economic collapse." We are facing further educational decline, and the decline of the inner cities, including areas of most major cities, where even the police fear to go. Gangs are growing, showing up in smaller cities at an alarming rate. America is in bad shape. Even if it's still in good shape compared to most other countries, we are still in serious decline. The answers are not coming from our leaders to solve these problems. We are all very concerned.

The curious thing is that when you study the Gallup Polls and the Barna Group Polls and the Harris Polls, etc.; you find that America claims to be Christian. Fifty percent, 60 percent, 70 percent, confess to be Christian. Why is there so little Christian impact? If a great majority of us are believers, why is there so little influence on our culture?

Barna, in his book, *The Frog in the Kettle,* describes his findings under the heading "What Americans think it means to be a Christian." Only 19 percent of Americans think to be a Christian means to accept Christ as Savior and to have a personal relationship with Jesus. Twenty-two percent say they don't know what being a Christian means. Twenty-one percent say it is to live differently than other people. Fourteen percent say being a Christian means to love others and help other people. Fourteen percent say to believe in God. Ten percent say being a Christian means to be a good person. Imagine, 22 percent admit they don't understand what being a Christian means![1] Since surveys are dated, it's probably worse by now. One explanation of these startling statistics is that few of those who think they are Christians truly are believers in the finished work of Christ.

The gospel has been preached in America for years, and we are down to only 19 percent that understand what being a Christian means.

Some would say our problem, as Christians, is that we are not socially active enough. We are not involved in dealing with the problems in this culture in a frontal, direct, and involved way. They would advocate civil disobedience, writing your congressman, making phone calls, and any number of political action steps. They claim we need to get out of the pulpit, out of the pew, and into the streets with our Christianity—into the streets for social action and impact.

The problem is that a great portion of what's being said about social activism, issues, and political concerns is actually centered on very serious issues. They are issues of deep concern to anyone who is morally awake. However, simply preaching the gospel, and simply becoming more socially active are both far short of the biblical ideal.

The reason there is so little Christian impact in our day is that we do not know our role as citizens of Heaven. We are citizens of Heaven and God has us here for a reason, yet we often do not have a clue about what we are to do. Saving more people, alone, is not the answer. Social cause Christianity is cultural. It is not a biblical response. The Christian social cause approach is an attempt to effect change through a particular strategy that is cultural, not biblical. There is a growing number who see the bankruptcy of "Christian politics" and are putting our voices together to call the Church back to authentic Christianity and true impact.

Our cause-orientation damages both our churches and our personal Christianity. Another paragraph from Barna's book reads:

Finally, since churches rely heavily upon volunteers, we must keep in mind that during the 90's, sacrificing time to help the church will rate as a lower priority to many people. We'll become more cause-driven, responding to critical social and political issues. Can the church portray the spiritual emptiness of many people's lives as an issue worth committing to? Can we create the aura of Christianity as a contemporary movement that is reshaping the value-structure of America after several decades of decadence and demise? Churches able to do such things will find a plentiful field of volunteers to call upon for various ministries. The key to maintaining those people will be the effective communication and celebration of the positive, tangible results of their efforts. The carrot at the end of the stick will be vivid demonstrations of the church's impact on individual lives, the community, and our nation.[2]

Barna seems to concede the issue of causes and being cause-driven, suggesting that we need to make church a cause. That may be part of the answer. It is a graphic cultural agenda for people to have a cause and fight for it. I'm going to suggest that the answer is to return to authentic Christianity, which locally finds itself best expressed in an authentic church, which is simply a local family of Heavenly citizens following God's plan for impact.

The Book of Hebrews is concerned with people abandoning their Christianity and returning to the religion of their fathers, which was a Judaistic, legalistic system. Chapter 11 is the chapter of faith.

The definition of faith begins in verse 1. "Now faith is the substance of things hoped for, the evidence of things not seen." This entire chapter deals with faith. In the middle of it we find verse 8 picking up the life of Abraham.

> *By faith Abraham obeyed when he was called to go out to the place which he would afterward receive as an inheritance. And he went out, not knowing where he was going. By faith he sojourned in the land of promise as in a foreign country, dwelling in the tents with Isaac and Jacob, the heirs with him of the same promise.* (Hebrews 11:8-9)

> *These all died in faith, not having received the promises, but having seen them afar off were assured of them, embraced them, and confessed that they were strangers and pilgrims on the earth. For those who say such things declare plainly that they seek a homeland. And truly if they had called to mind that country from which they had come out, they would have had opportunity to return. But now they desire a better, that is, a heavenly country. Therefore God is not ashamed to be called their God, for He has prepared a city for them.* (Hebrews 11:13-16)

Though the Church is distinctly God's heavenly people, the author of Hebrews rightly illustrates the "alien status" of all who follow God in any age.

Abraham typifies this sojourning in the world in a graphic way.

They walked by faith. They were pilgrims and aliens wherever they lived. It was not their home. They had not fully received their home and the writer of Hebrews explains that they were looking beyond to a Heavenly home. F.F. Bruce writes:

> It was Abraham, Isaac and Jacob, however, who lived preeminently as "strangers and pilgrims on the earth" in a sense which is inapplicable to those Israelites of later generations after the settlement in Canaan. To Abraham, Isaac and Jacob Canaan remained a "promised" land to the end of their days; their descendants saw the fulfillment of what was a promise to the patriarchs. But to the patriarchs that promise was sure, because it was God's promise; and they staked everything on its certainty. In one sense, as our author has stated earlier, Abraham, "having patiently endured ... obtained the promise" (Heb. 6:15)—he obtained the promised son, not only by his birth but also by his restoration from death "in a figure", as verse 19 puts it—but the full realization of the promises had to await the day of Christ. "I'm a stranger and a sojourner with you", said Abraham to the sons of Heth (Gen. 23:4); he recognized and accepted his status as a pilgrim. So too Jacob, in old age, speaks of the long course of

his life as "the days of the years of my pilgrimage" (Gen. 47:9).[3]

These men looked ahead to the promises of God and had not yet received them. Though the history and the events of this story line are important, I want to offer an outline which is more application oriented.

This section of Hebrews includes two calls and a result. The first call is the call of the citizen of Heaven to walk by faith. It is a walk by faith in five ways. First, the call of the citizen of Heaven is to walk by faith unto death. "These all died in faith, not having received the promises but having seen them afar off..." (v. 13). These individuals understood that many of the promises of God will not be fulfilled during one's lifetime. Their attitude was a looking beyond, even past the option of death, looking for the fulfillment of the promises of God. Their faith was an anticipation and eternal hope unto death and beyond.

The second aspect of their call is that they saw the promise before it was fulfilled. Notice verse 13, "Having seen them afar off." They looked before the fulfillment. That is often the definition of faith. We tend to have faith in things that are actually seen, which is not faith at all. We try to build confidence in tangibles. Our car has worked every day. We've had it looked after, checked, and on a maintenance schedule, so we call it faith to get in and drive somewhere, thinking it will work. That is not faith in the way that the Word of God means faith. The Word of God means taking God at His word, seeing a promise, and looking beyond the fact that it is not yet fulfilled.

The third thing here, concerning this call of the citizen of Heaven and our walk of faith is the assurance of the promise. In verse 13 it states they "were assured of them." They were not only faithful unto death, not only looking ahead to something they didn't see, but there was an abiding assurance in them that this too would come to pass.

The fourth aspect is the embracing of the promises. Still in verse 13 is "embraced them." We see they died in faith. They didn't receive the promises. They were assured of them, and they embraced them. They took them as their own. They took them for themselves. This was an act of faith, of holding onto them, clinging to the promises of God.

Finally, and most interesting in this progression in verse 13 is the confession of being a pilgrim. They confessed that they were strangers and pilgrims on the earth. The person that walks by faith is a believer indeed. They had an active faith that was unto death, seeing the promise fulfilled, assured of the promise, embracing the promise, and confessing in agreement with God that they were pilgrims on the earth. This was not their country. This was not where they belonged. We need to ask:

Do we walk by faith in this way? Unto death? Seeing the promise before it is fulfilled? Assured of the promise? Embracing the promise? Confessing even ultimately to be a pilgrim on earth as a citizen of Heaven?

The call of the pilgrim on earth is two-fold. First, to desire and seek a homeland (v. 14). "For those who say such things declare plainly that they seek a homeland." They seek a homeland. Look at verse 16a, "But now they desire a better, that is, a heavenly country." In both regards, what's being said is that as we grow in this faith, we are to look and long for this Heavenly homeland, and this Heavenly country that is ours.

Recently, I counseled two friends. One called to say, "I want to go home to Heaven." Another was facing the possibility of a life-threatening surgery and said, "I want to stay on earth for awhile." I wanted them to swap attitudes. Everybody would have been happy. One would have had the opportunity to go be with the Lord, and the other would get to stay. Instead, we worked through it another way, and both of them embraced the grace to trust God for whatever time He keeps them here as we all are to do.

There is a natural desire to seek a homeland. If we know Christ, and grow up in Him, that desire must well up within. It must grow. It must be a part of what it means to be a Christian and a pilgrim here on the earth.

There's a second call to being a pilgrim, and that is to not remember or return to the old country. Verse 15 says, "And truly if they had called to mind that country from which they had come out, they would have had an opportunity to return." This is an important concept. The idea is that Abraham and the others left that country. They left Ur, a very advanced civilization, with plenty of luxury. Even in the midst of hardship, they did not think about what it was like back in Ur. They did not think about returning to that country. It was the nature of being a pilgrim. They no longer looked to that country as an answer for their sojourn and their time of faith on earth.

Following the path of a pilgrim on earth has a special effect. We have a call to be a citizen of Heaven and walk by faith, the call of the pilgrim on earth, and we finally have the result of fulfilling these callings. The result may surprise you: God is not ashamed. "But now they desire a better, that is, a heavenly country. Therefore God is not ashamed to be called their God..." (v. 16). God is not ashamed to be called the God of Abraham, the God of Isaac, the God of Jacob. God is not ashamed to be identified with these people. Would God be ashamed to be known as the God of Fred? The God of Mark? The God of Janet? The God of your local church?

F.F. Bruce adds an interesting comment to all of this when he says:

> The truth is, their true homeland was not on earth at all. The better country on which they had set their hearts was the heavenly country. The earthly Canaan and the earthly Jerusalem were but temporary object-lessons pointing to the saints' everlasting rest, the well-founded city of God. Those who put their trust in God receive a full reward, and that reward must belong not to this transient world-order but to the enduring order which participates in the life of God. The example of the patriarchs is intended to guide the readers of the epistle to a true sense of values; like the elect sojourners of the Dispersion addressed in I Peter, they are to live in this world as "aliens and exiles" (I Pet. 2:11, RSV), and like the Philippians to whom Paul wrote, their "citizenship is in heaven" (Phil. 3:20). This ideal has proved too high for many Christians throughout the centuries of our era; yet there has never failed a distinguished succession of men and women possessed of this pilgrim attitude who have sung with Henry Francis Lyte:

> *"It is not for me to be seeking my bliss*
> *And building my hopes in a region like this;*
> *I look for a city which hands have not piled,*
> *I pant for a country by sin undefiled."* [4]

Kenneth Wuest also offers us a very insightful quote from history. He says, "In the anonymous Epistle to Diagnetus, probably of the second century, there occur these words concerning Christians: 'They inhabit their own country, but as sojourners: they take part in all things as citizens, and endure all things as aliens: every foreign country is theirs, and every country is foreign.' "[5] That is what Christianity is about. We don't quite fit in this world, especially the more we grow in Christ.

I am concerned about the growing movement and focus on saving our country through government and social activism. I am concerned about this movement that has been going on for some time in Christianity that sees our mission as saving America. I'm concerned for five reasons.

First, *when we get caught in social activism, it is a focus on that old country*. The patriarchs did not return to the old country. Often, we look at history and long for the time when America was "Christian." We believe it to have been wonderful. Morality reigned and it was in the laws to read the Bible. One had to know the Bible to be admitted into Harvard. This was a wonderful time in Christianity, a pinnacle. The air was clear and the sky was blue, and Christianity shone as it should on earth. Yet here we are today in decay, ruin, devastation, moral collapse, bankruptcy, and lack of impact. This old country is calling to us to return.

We want to return to that country and reshape present-day America into that country again. However, this is not what God has called us to. Furthermore, the energy we put in trying to meet this goal runs the danger of putting us in such a position, surprisingly, that God will be ashamed to be called our God, according to the Bible.

My second concern is that *such a focus is unfitting for a pilgrim and displays little heart for Heaven.* If we get obsessed with earthly causes as pilgrims, we throw off our pilgrimage and own this country. We shift our focus to the idea that we belong here and focus on the tangible here and now. We then belong fully to an earthly country. The more we focus on it, the less we will on Heaven. I realize what I am saying about a Heavenly focus is foreign to many Christians because we are so concerned with the world and "Christian America." Yet, we are pilgrims and our hearts must be fixed on the things of Heaven.

My third concern is that *Christian activism is an unbiblical strategy for change.* In the New Testament era the civilized world was full of pagans. There was temple worship, which often included prostitution. There was gluttony such that people would gorge themselves, then go out and vomit so they could return to eat more. Everything there was bankrupt. There was no nuclear family. The wife was in one place, the mistress in another. It was a mess. It was insane. It was horrible. Religious freedom was given to everyone except those who would claim that their god was exclusive of all the others. Everybody had a god. Every city had a god.

Christians came in as aliens and strangers. They felt no compulsion to belong to the culture and they didn't have to participate in all the insanity. They loved each other, they embraced the grace of God, and they grew, learned, and were transformed. They reached out and shared with others this hope of having sin removed, a destiny secured, and a new community to belong to against the culture. They strove to walk sanely in an insane environment.

Christianity infiltrated the culture and grew. Men and women who knew Christ were raised up and placed in positions of power. Their strategy, though, was not to change the culture. The strategy was to share the grace of God with others and help them become fellow pilgrims toward Heaven. That was always the strategy. Every time Christianity finally took over a culture, however, it became confused and blended into that culture—losing its distinctiveness.

When Christianity merges with a culture, it begins to die. History faithfully records this cycle, but history never demands we repeat it.

The fourth concern I have with Christian activism is that *social causes strip our energy and lead us away from our true calling*. The energy that we put into social causes keeps us away from what the Word of God says we as believers need to be doing with one another, as well as for this lost and dying world. If you've ever tried to put your whole energy into something, you find you only have so much to give before it's depleted. Energy spent by the Christian ideally is spent on the clearly explained 'causes of God' for pilgrims on this earth. These causes are found in those things God's Word emphasizes the most. They are found in advancing the Church, sharing the Good News of God's grace, and in helping other Christians grow up in Christ. If believers did little more than follow the exhortations in the New Testament surrounding the phrase "one another," much of their responsibility before God would be fulfilled.

My fifth concern is that *intense, hyper-social activism breeds false hope and hopelessness because it is visible.* When we look at what we are doing, whether it is winning the pornography battle or winning any other temporal battle, we confuse our Christianity with earthly victories. Then our hope, if not our faith, dies. Romans 8:24 says that "hope that is seen is not hope." You don't hope in something you see. We also, as believers, are to walk by faith and not by sight according to Second Corinthians 5:7.

The most basic biblical understanding discerns the false hope found in focusing on earthly things. Being obsessed with social causes breeds hopelessness. Look at Hebrews 12:28:

Therefore, since we are receiving a kingdom which cannot be shaken, let us have grace, by which we may serve God acceptably with reverence and godly fear. (Hebrews 12:28)

When we are concerned about our true country, Heaven, a country that cannot be shaken, then we are focusing on it and our faith is not shaken. Ultimately our hope will be satisfied. It doesn't matter what we've done through history. Governments come and go, rise up and collapse, they do well and they do poorly. Still, they are under the prince of the power of the air. They are not of God, though ultimately controlled by Him.

If you focus on what you can do to change a government, your hope will go up and down. How does it feel with every Supreme Court decision about abortion and *Roe* v. *Wade*? It seems every positive decision is followed with a negative one. Where is your faith? Is your faith in the Supreme Court or the Supreme Being?

Some governments grow corrupt, kill innocent babies, oppress the poor, and oppress religious freedom. Are we to just do nothing and sit back?

Beloved, I beg you as sojourners and pilgrims abstain from fleshly lusts which war against the soul, having your conduct honorable among the Gentiles, that when they speak against you as evildoers, they may, by your good works which they observe, glorify God in the day of visitation. (I Peter 2:11-12)

Peter exhorts us to live honorable lives noted for good works. In Matthew 25, Christ observes that good works are on the order of giving water in His name and visiting prisoners. Picketing, civil disobedience, etc. are not what the New Testament writers had in mind when they spoke of good deeds.

Some ask, "What about government?" The Scriptures respond:

> *Therefore submit yourselves to every ordinance of man for the Lord's sake, whether to the king as supreme, or to governors, as to those who are sent by him for the punishment of evildoers and for the praise of those who do good. For this is the will of God, that by doing good you may put to silence the ignorance of foolish men—as free, yet not using your liberty as a cloak for vice, but as servants of God. Honor all people. Love the brotherhood. Fear God. Honor the king.* (I Peter 2:13-17)

What is the Christian response to government? It is to be about the business of what authentic Christianity is to be, embracing grace, serving others, and giving ourselves and resources over to Him. The only complaint against us is to be our good deeds. We are to submit to government, not fight against it.

There are two things to remember as a caution for clarity. If you are burdened for a social cause and want to be a part of it, God is not necessarily

124

against your being involved, provided you are primarily involved in fulfilling the Great Commission. If you are involved in passing on what you are learning spiritually to others, reaching out to the lost, and building up people who know the Savior so they can be encouraged; if you're doing that as your first priority, and God burdens you for a cause, go for it. Your life will be in balance that way. But, be careful. If you replace the Great Commission with your cause, you will step outside of the Word and will of God. The misguided energy that you put forth, I believe, could be a basis of God being ashamed to be called your God.

Second, for clarity, let me suggest that you can live out your calling. If you are called to serve in government or politics, serve to the glory of God. Praise God that He has raised you up, just like any other calling or vocation. However, never forget that this is not your real country; Heaven is. Don't get it confused.

Why do we fight for America? Why are we so burdened about America's future? Perhaps it has to do with our family and friends. We have always fought to protect them, we will fight to protect them, and we are to fight to protect them. But in large measure, it's just because we were born here. If you were born in Switzerland, you wouldn't be concerned about America. Are you concerned about

Ethiopia right now? You may be, but not in the same way as Ethiopians. Why? You weren't born there.

In conclusion, let's consider two examples. Many Christian leaders in our day believe that fighting for social causes is actually the way in which the Great Commission is fulfilled. They promote to us that authentic faith shows itself in social activity which, in turn, will impact the nation. We have attempted here to argue that this approach is spiritually inferior to the way in which God has most effectively impacted nations.

Consider this issue by placing yourself in a different place, in an imaginary time in history. It may be your own present city or town; however, think of it as completely unreached. The message of Christ has never been there. There is no knowledge of His name, His deeds, or the Bible. The people in this city are enslaved to various religions. These religions include the promotion of such things as worshiping idols, sacrificing animals, open prostitution, and homosexuality. Occasionally in this city it is even known that there are human sacrifices for special ceremonial events. The culture is vile and disease-ridden, both physically and spiritually. You have moved to this city, sent out from a church far away. You have come with six others who want to establish a church and impact this community. Religious freedom is permitted, though they certainly look on new ideas with some dismay, and yet also with some curiosity.

What would your strategy be to impact this city? Even a cursory understanding of the New Testament would lead you to one strategy. You would not begin to picket City Hall. You would not begin to have petitions signed to stop human and animal sacrifices. You would not circulate flyers condemning other religions. You and your other believing missionaries would begin to establish a church. Your focus would be to love each other and support each other as fellow strangers to that land. You would not only be strangers to the city, but you also would be strangers because you belong to Heaven. The strategy would be to labor faithfully among these people and, as opportunity arose, to share the message of God's grace and forgiveness in Jesus Christ. As God enabled, you would then begin to see others come to Christ and join in this "new" religion. Your focus would be to establish them in the Word of God that they too might share this message of the grace of God with others. Others would come and join the church. In the course of time, as the church grew, you would establish other churches within the area to continue the same process. Perhaps some government officials would come to faith. Perhaps the leaders of other religious groups would come to faith and they all, from their own conviction and

127

understanding of God's Word, begin to exert their influence for change.

In the course of time, the opinions and the popularity of the Christian message would reach deeply into the culture and move it to give up many practices it would never have considered giving up through political action. Your initial plan would not be to change the culture, but to reach and establish as many believers as you could in order to populate Heaven, understanding that the battle is a spiritual one, and the rewards and impact eternal.

Let me ask an important question. If this strategy is the superior strategy for that context, why would it be inferior in any other context? Why would the best plan for the worst place not work even better in a less "sinful" environment? Why wouldn't the best plan for a pagan culture work even more effectively in America today? Consider an illustration. What is the best way for a young man to win the affection of a young lady? Generally, we would say, "Bring flowers and gifts. Give compliments. Talk to her about what she's interested in, or just talk to her a lot! Win her through showering her with attention." If this strategy is the "best" one to win a young lady, how much more effective would it be toward a wife? If God gave us a strategy for a sinful world, why would we change strategies for different degrees of sin in a given country?

If your social cause or social action includes reaching unbelievers, then you are to be praised. If your social cause takes the place of the Church, then it is clearly less than God's best. If you are actively involved in growing up in the Lord with other citizens of Heaven as a part of reaching out to the spiritually lost and dying, then you can rest assured that you are about the business God has called us all to. No one's Christianity is inferior, nor without strategy, when it is focused on the clear mandate in the Word of God to live righteously and spread the Good News that Christ died for the sins of the world.

Someone might ask, "Isn't there a balance?"

Personally, perhaps. Theologically, no. There is no balance between Heaven and earth. No balance between the kingdom of light and the kingdom of darkness. No balance between the wisdom from above and earthly wisdom. An individual may find opportunites to advance the cause of Heaven through the providence of God as did Esther. Even organizations may find ways to blend their cause with fulfilling the Great Commission. Praise the Lord for His providential working and the creativity of the saints! Thinking, however, that political action divorced from biblical priorities is actually a means of advancing the Church is sorely misguided.

Balance, as a popular word in Christian circles, is also a very unbiblical concept when it means compromise—especially the compromise of truth.

Consider this contrast. Two individuals visit a Christian leader to share about their present involvements. The first is heavily involved in a particular cause which addresses a great moral sin. The goal of the cause is to "educate the public and encourage legislation to restrain this moral evil." A biblical leader would caution this individual in two ways. First he would exhort this person to maintain actions and strategies that follow the fruit of the Spirit (Gal. 5:22-23) and the wisdom from above (Jas. 3:17-18). Second, he would caution this person to be careful to not elevate this cause over the cause of Heaven. "If all of your energy and efforts in this cause displace your involvement in reaching out to the lost and building up the saints (Eph. 4:16; Heb. 10:24), then you are going to fall short of the clear direction of God's Word. This is 'just' a caution."

How about our second person? This individual comes to our Christian leader for advice also. This person has decided to focus strictly on what has traditionally been called evangelism and discipleship. The focus will be on walking with God, offering a neighborhood evangelistic Bible study, and teaching younger Christians how to understand the Bible for themselves. Could our Christian leader "caution" this person? Could he say, "That's all fine, but you better make sure that you're active in a social cause too!"? Of course, such a warning is preposterous. This individual is using his time and energy toward clearly biblical ends. A social cause would distract and exhaust him. This second person may not be much of an "American citizen" by current definitions, but he or she would be quite a citizen of Heaven. If there is a clear need of caution in one circumstance and no caution needed in the second, what does that reveal?

We can attempt to change people and countries through external moral, social, intellectual pressures; but this is not the way of God. God's way is to change the nation through changing her heart. The heart of a nation changes through the hearts of her citizens. It is solely the power of the gospel of the grace of God that brings this change. While legislation can only restrain, the message of Christ fully renews.

Of course, God's will has never been to simply "change a nation," but to populate and establish a new and perfect one in the age to come.

The reality is that governments come and go. *We are spiritually reborn into another nation, and our responsibility as pilgrims is to walk with Christ, establish our hearts in grace, and reach out to and embrace others, moving them from the kingdom of darkness to the kingdom of light. We must establish them in a loving fellowship, a church, that is travelling against the current of culture toward Heaven.*

The leaders of churches all over America are looking for a few good citizens of Heaven, saints who see Heaven as their country and would like to change the world by joining together as pilgrims, to show the world the power of real Christianity the way it's supposed to work. The way it always has in every situation that God used it.

Lord, even before You, my understanding may be skewed and wrong. Yet as I've wrestled on this very idea, I affirm before You that I still don't want You to be ashamed in any sense of my walk before You because I was misdirected, sacrificing the best on the altar of the good. Lord, I hate it that babies are killed, I hate it that pornography and addiction proliferates in this country. I hate it that people are enslaved to the inner city. They have no real hope of getting out. I hate it that education is going down the tubes and the population is more illiterate than ever. Oh God, there is so much I hate about this country, and there is is much I love about it. Yet before You, I want to know a heart that sees a Heavenly country, that this isn't all there is. As a pilgrim with the others You are raising up, I would like to be about Your business of doing good and sharing the grace of God. Changing the world one life at a time. Move in our hearts as citizens of Heaven to go against the culture, to be a lifeboat, to take as many as we can with us to that Heavenly place You've prepared for us. Amen.

For here we have no continuing city [country], but we seek the one to come. (Hebrews 13:14)

Endnotes

Chapter 4

1. Kenneth S. Wuest, *Wuest's Word Studies from the Greek New Testament*. Grand Rapids, MI: Wm. B. Eerdmans, 1973, 1:217.

2. Curtis Vaughan, "Colossians," p. 209 Taken from the book, THE EXPOSITOR'S BIBLE COMMENTARY, VOL 11 edited by Frank Gaebelain. Copyright © 1978, by the Zondervan Corporation. Used by permission.

3. Ibid.

4. Ibid.

Chapter 5

1. Martin Bolt and David G. Myers, *The Human Connection: How People Change People*. Downers Grove, IL: InterVarsity Press, 1984, pp. 84-85.

2. Ibid.

3. Ibid., p. 87.

4. Ibid., pp. 92-93.

Chapter 6

1. Robert S. McGee, *The Search for Significance,* 2nd ed. Houston and Dallas, TX: Rapha Publishing/Word Inc., 1990, pp. 73-74.

Chapter 7

1. George Barna, *The Frog in the Kettle.* Ventura, CA: Gospel Light/Regal Books Div., 1990, p. 114. Used by permission.

2. Ibid., p. 96.

3. F.F. Bruce, *The Epistle to the Hebrews.* Grand Rapids, MI: Wm. B. Eerdmans, 1964, p. 304.

4. Ibid., pp. 305-306.

5. Kenneth S. Wuest, *Wuest's Word Studies from the Greek New Testament.* Grand Rapids, MI: Wm. B. Eerdmans, 1973, 2:203.